André Previn's
Guide to Music

André Previn's Guide to Music

Edited by André Previn

MACMILLAN LONDON

Text by: Neil Ardley, Richard Balkwill, Clifford Bevan, Michael Hurd, Jannet King and Alyn Shipton

Designed by: Julian Holland

Artwork by:
David Baird, Brian and Constance Dear, Oxford Illustrators, Nancy Petley-Jones

Text © Macmillan Publishers Ltd 1983
Introduction © André Previn 1983

First published in hardback 1983 by
MACMILLAN LONDON LIMITED
4 Little Essex Street London
WC2R 3LF and Basingstoke

Associated companies in Auckland, Dallas, Delhi, Dublin, Hong Kong, Johannesburg, Lagos, Manzini, Melbourne, Nairobi, New York, Singapore, Tokyo, Washington and Zaria

ISBN 0 333 33978 9

Printed in Hong Kong

Photograph acknowledgements

Strings

3 *l* Bildarchiv Foto Marburg; *r* National Gallery, London; **4** *bl* British Library, London; *r* Clive Barda, London; **5** David Redfern, London; **6** *l* Photographie Giraudon, Paris; *b* Bildarchiv Preussicher Kulturbesitz, Berlin; **7** *t* Albert Cooper, Winchester; *b* Minao Shibata, Tokyo; **8** *t* Camilla Jessel, London; *b* Clive Barda; **9** Victoria & Albert Museum, London; **10** *l* Clive Barda; *m* Royal Academy of Arts, London; *r* Romilly John, Fordingbridge/photo Tate Gallery, London; **11** *t* Alix B Williamson, New York; *br* Landesmuseum für Geschichte und Volkstum/photo Otto Hoppe; **12** Camilla Jessel; **13** David Redfern; **14** Patrimonie Nacional, Madrid; **15** *bl* Eric Auerbach, London; *br* London Features International; **16** *t* Deutsche Staatsbibliothek, Berlin; *b* Hamburger Kunsthalle; **17** *l* Rola Music, Cheltenham/photo Brian Donnan; *r* David Redfern; **18** *tl, l, r* International Institute for Comparative Music Studies and Documentation, Berlin/photos Manfred Junius, Alain Daniélow; *br* Jean Jenkins, London; **19** *t* British Library; *b* Metropolitan Museum of Art, New York; **20** Hunterian Collection, Glasgow University; **21** *t* Camilla Jessel; *bl* International Institute for Comparative Music Studies and Documentation, Berlin/photo H H Touma; *r* Musée de l'Homme, Paris; *tl* David Redfern; *tr* Deutsche Gramophon; *b* John Levy Collection, School of Scottish Studies, Edinburgh

Woodwind

29 *b* Nippon Gakki Co Ltd, Japan; **30** *tl* Horniman Museum, London; *tr* Horace Fitzpatrick; *bl* Klaus Wachsmann, Tisbury; **31** *tl* National Gallery of Art (Samuel H Kress Collection), Washington DC; *bl* Soprintendenza alle Gallerie e alle Opere d'Arte, Venice/photo Osvaldo Böhm; *br* Bayerisches National- museum, Munich; **32** *t* Dolmetsch Musical Instruments/photo Simon Futcher Photographics, Haslemere; *b* Grosvenor Museum, Chester; **33** *tl* Dolmetsch Musical Instruments/photo Simon Futcher Photographics; *bl*

Hispavox S A, Madrid; Bate Collection, Oxford; **34** *t* Judith Pearce/photo Misha Donat; *l* Musées Nationaux, Paris; **36** Bernard Long, Essex; **37** Bill Lewington Ltd, London; **38** Popperfoto, London; **39** André Sas, Paris; **40** Ingpen & Williams Ltd; **41** *tl* Drawing by Gerard Hoffnung, published by Dobson Books, *b* Camilla Jessel, London; **42** *l* William Water- house; *r* Camilla Jessel; **43** *l* Royal Pavilion, Art Gallery and Museum, Brighton; *m* Mansell Collection, London and Alinari, Florence; *r* Deutsches Museum, Munich; **45** British Library; **48** *t* Camera Press, London; *m* Peter Cooke, Edinburgh; *b* Whispering Wind Band, leader Nicholas Bucknall/photo John Clark

Brass

50 *tl* British Dental Association, London; *b* Vincent Bach Corporation, Indiana; **51** *t* C G Conn Ltd, Indiana; *l* Boosey & Hawkes, London; *r* Paxman, London; *b* E H Tarr; **52** *tl* Bernard Long, Essex; *b* Conservatoire National Supérieur de Musique, Paris; **55** *tl/tr* Nationalmuseeet, Copenhagen; *b* Deutsches Archäologisches Institut, Rome; **56** Horniman Museum, London/ photo Bruce Scott, London; **57** *tl* Bate Collection, Oxford: *tr* Conservertoire National Supérieur de Musique/photo Publimages; *bl* National Museum, Prague; *br* Swiss National Tourist Board; **58** *tl* The Mansell Collection, London; *b* Germanisches National- museum, Nuremburg; **59** *tl* Drawing by Gerard Hoffnung, published by Dobson Books, Durham; *b* Vincent Bach Corporation; **60** *tl* Bate Collection, Oxford; *b* Boosey & Hawkes, London; **61** *tl* David Redfern, London; *bl* Ministry of Industry, Trade and Tourism, Jerusalem; *br* Philip Bate, London; **62** Drawing by Gerard Hoffnung, published by Dobson Books; **64** *tl* David Redfern, *b* Boosey & Hawkes; **65** Boosey & Hawkes; **66** *tl* Drawing by Gerard Hoffnung, published by Dobson Books; *b* Camilla Jessel, London; **67** *tl* Staatliches Institut für Musikforschung Preussicher Kulturbesitz, Musik- instrumenten-Museum, Berlin; *b* Faber & Faber, London; **68** *tl* Camilla Jessel;

b Willie Cornish Collection; **69** *tl* Gebrüder Alexander, Mainz; *m* Rudall, Carte & Co Ltd, London; *br* Norlin Music (UK) Ltd, Chelmsford; **71** Vincent Bach Corporation; **72** *tl* Public Relations, London District; *tr* Salvation Army, London; *b* Peter Cooke, Edinburgh

Percussion
79 Camilla Jessel, London; **80** *bm, br,* 9 br Musée de l'Homme, Paris; **81** *t* Camilla Jessel; **82** *tl* Drawing by Gerard Hoffnung, published by Dobson Books; *br* Paul Wood, London; **83** *l* Horniman Museum, London; *r* Camilla Jessel; **84** *tl* London District, Public Relations *br* Camilla Jessel; **85** *tr* Camilla Jessel; *br* Premier, Leicester; **86** *tl* Premier; *bl* Barnaby's Picture Library, London; **87** *tr* Koninklijk Museum voor Schone Kunsten, Antwerp/photo ACL, Brussels; **88** *tl* Musée de l'Homme, Paris; *b* Camilla Jessel; **89** London District, Public Relations; **90** *tl* Premier; *b* Jim Rosellini, California; **91** *t* Linda O'Brien, California; *b* Fitz Park Museum, Keswick; **92** *tl* Ludwig Drum Co, Chicago; *b* Camilla Jessel; **94** Camilla Jessel; **94** *t* Kensington News and Post, London; *b* Department of Information, Jakarta; **95** *t* Premier; *b* Robert Ellis, London

Keyboard instruments
98 *tl* The Duke of Rutland and the Roxburghe Club; **99** *tl* Towarzystwo imieria Fryderyka Chopin, Warsaw/ photo Mansell Collection, London; *tr* British Library; *b* Smithsonian Institute, Washington, DC; **102** *bl* Rheinisches Landesmuseum, Trier; *br* Jean Perrot, Moulincourt par Ully St Georges; **103** *tl* Giraudon, Paris; *br* Memlingmuseum, Bruges/photo ACL; **104** *r* N P Mander Ltd, London/photo Sydney W Newberry, Surrey; **105** *t* Malcolm Crowthers, London; *b* N P Mander Ltd/photo Sydney W Newberry; **106** *tl* British Library; *b* Graham Rankin, Chawton/photo Julian Holland; **108** *tl* Worcester Art Museum, Massachusetts; **109** *m* Germanisches Nationalmuseum, Nuremberg; *b* Victoria and Albert Museum, London; **110** *l* Royal College of Music, London; *r* Morley Galleries, London; **111** *tl* Francis Hauert, New York; *bl* Instituição José Relvas, Alpiarça; **112** Musikinstrumenten-

Museum, Karl-Marx-Universität, Leipzig; **113** *tl* Gesellschaft der Musikfreunde, Vienna; *b* Offentliche Kunstammlung, Basle; **114** Steinway & Sons, Long Island City, New York; **115** Max Jones, London; **116** *l* Camilla Jessel, London; *r* Keith Rowe/photo Stephanie Evans, London; **117** Clive Barda, London; *tr* Decca International; *bl* David Redfern, London; **118** *b* Camilla Jessel; **119** *t* A J Heuwekemeijer, Amsterdam; *b* University of Michigan, Ann Arbor

Voice
123 *t* Stuart-Liff Collection/Tunbridge Wells; *bl* Vlatko Dabac, Zagreb; *br* Mahi Ismail; **124** Clive Barda, London; **125** *t m* Clive Barda; *b* Malcolm Crowthers, London; **126** *tl* Bibliotèque Royale Albert 1er, Brussels; *bl* Verlag Peter Lang AG, Berne; *r* Victoria and Albert Museum, London; **127** *tl* Bibliotèque Nationale, Paris; *bl* Bibliotèque Municipale, Arras; *br* Bibliotèque Nationale, Paris; **128** British Library; **129** *l* Giraudon, Paris; *r* Hamlyn Group Picture Library, London; **130** and **131** Novello & Co Ltd., London; **132** *l* photo Musées Nationaux, Paris; *r* English National Opera, London; **133** *l* Guy Gravett, E Sussex; *r* Mander & Mitchenson, London; **134** Richard-Wagner-Gedenkstätte, Bayreuth; *tl* D'Oyly Carte, London; *bl* CBS Inc, New York; English National Opera, London; **138** *tl* Topic Records; *bl* Estate of Béla Bartók, Cedarhurst, New York; *br* English Folk Dance and Song Society, London; **131** *tl* Osian Ellis, London; *b* School of Scottish Studies, Edinburgh; **140** *tl* Paul Oliver; *bl* The Beinecke Rare Book and Manuscript Library, Yale University; *b* Paul Oliver; **141** *tl* Val Wilmer, London; **141** *b* David Redfern, London; **143** *tr bl* Verve; *br* David Redfern; **143** *tl* Camera Press Ltd, London; *l* London Photo Agency Ltd, London; *br* Melody Maker; **144** David Redfern

Electronic and mechanical
146 *tl* Historisches Museum, Basel; *b* Mansell Collection, London; **147** *br* British Library; *r* Alexandr Buchner; **148** and **149** The British Piano Museum, a Charitable Trust, Brentford; **150** *l* Rosetti Ltd, London; *b* Val Wilmer, London; **151** *l* Rosetti Ltd; *br* London Features International;

152 *tl* Summerfield, Gateshead; *b* photo Ashley Summerfield; **153** *t* LFI; *b* Equipment by Concert Sound; **154** *tl* Hammond, Milton Keynes; *b* Val Wilmer; **155** Hammond; **157** Yamaha, Hamamatsu; **158** *tl* Peter Loughran, High Wycombe; *b* David Crombie, London; **159** *tl* David Crombie; *b* LFI; **160** *tl* LFI; *b* Daily Telegraph, London/photo M Goddard; **161** *tl* BBC Photo Library, London; *b* Daily Telegraph, London; **162** *tl* Val Wilmer; *b* Camilla Jessel, London; **163** *tl* Philippe Coqueux, France; *b* Harman UK, Slough; **164** R Fassey, Villemomble; **165** John Clark, London; **166** *tl* Syco Systems Ltd, London/ photo Zefa Picture Library (UK) Ltd, London; *b* Casio; **167** Malcolm Crowthers, London; **168** *tl* Chris Davies, Network, London; *tr* Peter Loughran; *b* LFI

Composing, performing, recording
170 *tl* Camera Press, London; *b* BBC Hulton Picture Library; **171** *tl* Sarolta Kodály, Budapest; *m* Collection Viollet, Paris; *b* Popperfoto, London; **172** Max Jones, London; **173** Stravinsky Estate, New York/Meyer Collection, Paris; **174** *t* Staatliche Museen Preussischer Kulturbesitz, Musikabteilung, Berlin; *b* BBC Copyright; **175** *tl* British Library; *b* Novello & Co Ltd, London; **176** *tl* Gesellschaft der Musikfreunde, Vienna; Clive Barda, London; **177** Clive Barda; **178** *l* Malcolm Crowthers, London; *t* Reg Wilson, London; *b* Camilla Jessel, London; **182** London Symphony Chorus/photo John Clark; **180** Clive Barda; **181** *l* G Henle Verlag, Munich and H Stürtz AG, Würzburg; *bm* Breitkopf & Härtel (London) Ltd; *br* Boosey & Hawkes Ltd, London; **183** *l* Armando dal Molin, Oyster Bay, NY; *r* Music Print Corporation, Boulder, Colorado; **185** Performing Right Society, London; **186** Malcolm Crowthers; **187** *tl* Deutsches Gramophon/Malcolm Crowthers; *bl br* Camilla Jessel; **188** *tl* The Bettmann Archive Inc, New York; *ml* Jazz Music Books; *b* Max Jones, London; **181** *tl* Otto F Hess Collection, New York Public Library; *ml* Max Jones; *br* David Redfern; **190** *tl* William P Gottlieb, New York; *b* David Redfern; **191** *tl* Novello & Co Ltd; *b* National Film Archives Stills Library; **192** *tl* Popper-foto; *tr* Clive Barda; *b* Camera Press

Contents

Introduction

It seems to me that books on music, especially on the technical aspects of music and musical instruments, tend to be either so simple as to bore any bright six year old, or so crammed with the arcane as to baffle all but the most seasoned professional. In this volume we have tried very hard to hit the target somewhere in between these two extremes. Interesting but not complicated, informative but not professorial, easy to comprehend but not infantile. The text, the photos, the illustrations and the examples have all been written and chosen with this goal in mind.

This book covers a multitude of subjects and, hopefully, will furnish the answers to a lot of questions. Certainly it is a reference book, but one which is not meant to gather dust on the shelf next to your copy of *Pottery in Lapland*. Rather it is one which can either be picked up purposefully or casually dipped into. The families of instruments are covered thoroughly, both generically and individually; there are explanations of how the various instruments actually work and produce sounds. Five sections (Strings, Woodwind, Brass, Percussion and Keyboard instruments) have glossaries which define technical terms. There are a great many photographs of performers, and we must thank the Royal Philharmonic Orchestra and the BBC Symphony Orchestra for allowing their rehearsals to be invaded by cameras. We have included pertinent quotes from composers, and interviews were conducted especially for this book for which we must also thank Christopher Bishop, Nicola Lefanu, John McCabe, Andrzej Panufnik and Nina Walker for giving up their time.

I like to think that there are almost no limits to the various aspects of music, and so it would be conceited to believe that a single volume can examine all of them. But you *will* find a great catholicity of genres and styles discussed, from the medieval period through most of the types of classical music, right up to electronic instruments and compositional techniques. Jazz has not been overlooked, and neither has folk music. There is even a glancing look at the ubiquitous world of rock, a world to which I personally feel alien and in which, frankly, I am uninterested. But I am realistic enough to realise that trying to disregard it completely would be almost like pretending not to see the litter in the streets.

I suppose the one thing no book in the world can instil is a true and genuine love for music. That comes from listening, not reading. I use the word 'listening' as opposed to 'hearing' because hearing is passive and listening is active. You can 'hear' music in today's world without paying much attention to it. In waiting rooms, in office-building lifts, on planes, and in restaurants and department stores. Many young people wear earphones so much that I would not be surprised it they had to have them removed by surgery, and yet the chances are they are only hearing, and not listening. It is as if an already nerve-racked society had come to the conclusion that any moments of silence must be avoided. Real listening is something that has to be practised; it does not always come naturally. It is undeniable that some people listen better than others. It is a talent, and like all talents, can be nurtured. Practising this talent is a totaly selfless endeavour and without material reward. Instrumentalists enter competitions, runners try for the Olympics, composers seek commission, tennis players dream of Wimbledon. But there is no money in listening; there are nor medals or even compliments. It is its own reward.

Music can stir the imagination more deeply than any other art form, can cause tears or apprehension or smiles, prod the memory, reawaken ambition, stimulate or relax. It is wonderful to be aware of the fact that no two people sitting in a concert audience are going through the same thought processes. Of course, the whole thing is made so much easier by a small amount of technical knowledge about music. Listening does pay a certain kind of enormous dividend. Falling in love with music is a lifetime experience. It will give you pleasure, joy, comfort, exultation, and peace. Once music becomes a necessity and not just something to fill a momentary void, it will enrich your life beyond measure.

Strings

1 electric guitar
2 Spanish guitar
3 bass guitar
4 lute
5 sitar
6 mandolin
7 banjo
8 hurdy-gurdy
9 violin
10 viola
11 cello
12 double bass
13 viola da gamba
14 harp
15 zither

Here are the string instruments. They all look very different, but there are three main groups or "families:" the violin family, the guitar family and the harp family.

All the instruments have strings to make their sound, but each family makes that sound in a different way.

I

What makes the sound?

What are strings?

A string is a thin length of gut, silk, nylon or metal, which is stretched between two supports and free to vibrate. It is this vibration which makes a sound that our ears can hear.

How do they make a noise?

On their own, vibrating strings don't make much noise. They need a *soundboard* to *amplify* their vibrations into a sound we can hear easily.

To see how a soundboard works, try this experiment with an elastic band:

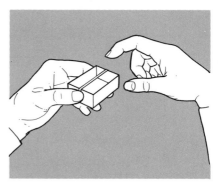

1 Stretch it between your fingers, and ask someone to pluck it.

2 Now stretch it over an open-topped cardboard box. Pluck it. Listen to the difference in sound.

Instruments of the violin and guitar family generally use this principle of a hollow box with *soundholes*, and strings stretched over it. As the strings vibrate, the box – or *body* – of the instrument and the air inside it start to *resonate*. The type, size and shape of the box, and both the length and quality of the strings produce the characteristic tone of an instrument. In the diagram of the parts of a violin you can see how sophisticated the structure of the soundbox has become.

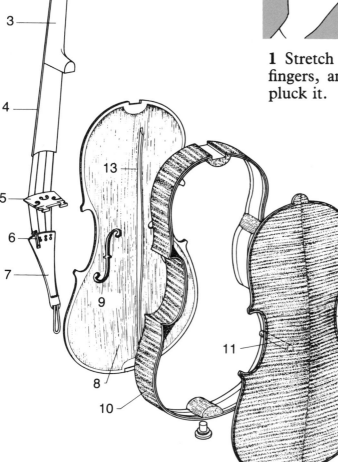

Parts of the violin
1 scroll; **2** pegs; **3** neck; **4** fingerboard; **5** bridge;
6 fine-tuner; **7** tailpiece; **8** top plate (belly);
9 soundhole (f-hole); **10** ribs; **11** soundpost;
12 back plate; **13** bass bar

The violinist draws the bow across the strings with the right hand.

The earliest instruction to pluck the strings of a bowed instrument is in Monteverdi's *Il Combattimento die Tancredi e Clorinda* of 1624, telling players to put the bow aside and 'pluck the strings with two fingers'.

'The Singing Lute Player' shows how the player's right hand plucks the strings.

How do the notes change?

There are three things about strings which make them produce different notes: tension, thickness and length. The looser, the thicker and the longer the string – the lower the note. This is because length, thickness and low tension make a string vibrate *slowly*. A few, slow, vibrations make a low note.

Think about the note of a motor-bike engine. The pitch changes as the engine parts move faster and vibrate more.

So the shorter, thinner and tighter the string, the higher the note.

How can you make different sounds?

Plucking The strings are plucked with the fingers, or struck using a *plectrum* held between first finger and thumb. As they are struck the strings sound and the note continues to resonate via the soundbox. Single notes or chords can be played.

Bowing The player draws the bow across the strings (making contact with one or two at a time) and the movement of the bow sets each string in vibration. As long as the bow is moving the strings will sound.

Violin

In 1756 Leopold Mozart wrote a book on playing the violin. Up until then people used to rest the violin on their chest, not their shoulder.

But this had its disadvantages: 'During quick movements of the hand, the violin has no support, and must therefore necessarily fall down.' Here is Leopold Mozart showing how to play with the violin tucked under the chin.

The modern violin has many 'voices' – it takes part in all kinds of music in different settings. Folk, jazz and classical musicians all use it and play it in their own particular style. But when the violin first came to be used, in the early sixteenth century, it was a folk-music instrument, and was heard at dances, weddings or mummer's plays.

Modern classical violinists hold the instrument under their chin, like this:

Notice two things, the bow, and the position of the player's left hand.

It is the left hand which produces notes of a different *pitch*. It changes the notes.

The violin's four strings each have a different note, tuned by pegs and fine adjusters. By placing a finger on a string the player shortens the length of string that's free to vibrate, and produces a higher sound. This is called a *stopped note*, whilst a string which is not stopped by the player's fingers is called an *open string*.

A player using an electric *pickup* to amplify the sound of the bowed violin

Profile
Size: 60 cm
Made of: pine, ebony; metal or gut strings
Bow: c72 cm long, pernambuco wood, nylon or horsehair
Sound made by: bowing or plucking
First example: c1510

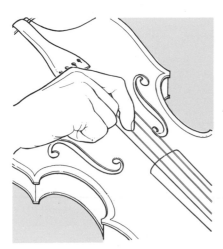

The player's right hand actually makes the sound. This is done either with a bow, or by plucking.

Bow The bow is rather like the type of bow used by an archer, except that the 'string' of the bow is made from hundreds of strands of horsehair and it can be tightened with a special mechanism, shown in the diagram.

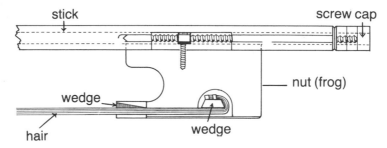

The horsehair is rubbed with resin (or *rosin*) from a fir tree, to make it sticky. Then it is drawn across the strings of the violin like this.

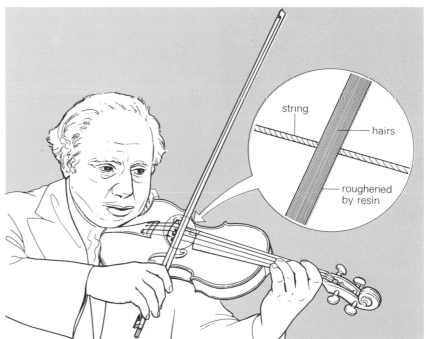

You can see from the close-up how the rough, sticky horsehairs make the violin string vibrate. The speed, direction and movement of the bow can be controlled, and allow the player to make long or short notes, and rough or smooth sounds.

Plucking The player can make a different sound by plucking the violin strings with the fingers of the right hand. This is called *pizzicato* and produces a very short sharp note.

An angel playing a rebec, painted in the early 16th century. The bow is a different shape from that used by modern violinists.

In 1672 one of the first great violinists was Nicola Matteis. His audience was full of wonder at him and his way of performing. He was a very tall and large-bodied man, using a very long bow, who 'rested his instrument against his short ribs, and with that could hold an audience by the ears longer than the ordinary, and not a whisper heard amongst them.'

No-one knows who invented the violin; it developed from a number of instruments in use about 450 years ago. One of its early ancestors was the rebec.

Unlike the violin, the rebec never developed into a standardised instrument: all sorts of shapes and sizes existed with anything from one to five strings. The first violins were sometimes referred to as little rebecs – 'rebechini' – and both instruments had rather harsh voices, being described at the time as 'tasteless and vulgar'.

As the violin was developed into an instrument with a more refined tone, the rebec remained an instrument of the people. In fact, this class distinction was turned into law in France when street fiddlers were ordered to play the rebec and not the violin in 1742.

Both early violins and rebecs were held 'along the arm', or rested on the chest. The introduction of the modern playing position made the violin suitable for more complicated music. Composers started to write for it, as players became able to play more in tune, and more quickly. The rebec, however, because of its deeply rounded shape could only be held in the less convenient old-fashioned position.

Dancing masters used another type of violin. This miniature version became known as the pocket violin or kit.

Dancing master of 1745 holding a kit in his left hand

In an orchestra, there are more violins than any other instrument. This is because there are two sections, the 'firsts' and the 'seconds'. Every section of the orchestra has a *principal* who is responsible for that section. The principal of the first violins is known as the *leader* or *concert master* of the orchestra. He or she comes on stage alone just before the conductor at the beginning of a concert. At the end of a piece the two shake hands, since the leader symbolises the entire orchestra.

A huge variety of classical music has been written for the violin, both as a solo instrument and as part of an orchestra. One of its settings as a solo instrument is in a *concerto* where it is accompanied by an orchestra.

It is a popular instrument for children to learn but to play it properly is hard for most people, and takes a long time. A Japanese, Shin'ichi Suzuki has developed a method of teaching the violin to whole classes of very young children. They all learn together and give performances involving as many as 3000 violinists.

The virtuoso Paganini who was alive in the last century. He was so brilliant that people thought he was in league with the devil!

Below: Shin'ichi Suzuki listens to the sound made by each of the children in his class to make sure they are playing in tune.

Viola

Profile

Size: c 70 cm long

Made of: wood with gut or metal strings

Bow: c 75 cm long

Sound made by: bowing or plucking

First example: c1510–30

The viola looks much the same as a violin, especially as it's played in the same way and held under the chin. But it's slightly bigger in every dimension. The body is wider and deeper, and the strings are longer and thicker. Because of this it makes a lower sound and the *tone* of the instrument is deeper and mellower.

Unlike the violin the viola is normally only used in classical music: in chamber groups and orchestras and as a solo instrument. In this string section of a symphony orchestra the violas (centre) are clearly larger than the violins (below).

How do players of instruments in the violin family know the correct position for the fingers of the left hand? Most players follow systems of fingering which group notes in particular places on the fingerboard, known as *positions*. These are learnt and carefully practised until the player can find any note with ease.

Left: A viola being played by Pinchas Zukerman, who makes appearances as a soloist on both this instrument and the violin

Early violas became famous for their deep and mournful tone. John Evelyn in 1679 wrote about their 'sweetness and novelty', whilst Mattheson in 1713 found them 'tender and languishing'. In France Rousseau thought the viola was too 'strident'.

Violas, though they are bigger than violins, vary considerably in size. The viola has often been considered inferior to the violin because it cannot achieve such a perfect sound and fewer pieces are written for it. However, the composer Mozart (himself an excellent violin and viola player) wrote a *Sinfonia concertante* in 1779 in which the two instruments share the role of soloist. More recently, in the nineteenth century, Berlioz wrote *Harold in Italy* in which the viola is a solo instrument. In this century many composers have written concertos for the viola, including Sir William Walton and Béla Bartók. Hindemith wrote several pieces for the unaccompanied instrument which, like Mozart, he performed himself.

Viola d'amore

A close relation of the viola, the viola d'amore usually has fourteen tuning pegs and a lion or cupid in place of the normal scroll. It was developed in the late seventeenth century. Its main difference from the modern viola is that it usually has seven playing strings and a further seven *sympathetic* strings which sound when the playing strings are bowed in the normal way. It has a sad and mournful tone and J S Bach often used it to represent crying or weeping. The viola d'amore was not used very often during the nineteenth century and has no place in the modern symphony orchestra. Recently, however, like other 'early' instruments, musicians have learnt to perform on it again.

Profile
Size: 80 cm long
Made of: wood
Strings: 14: 8 gut and 6 metal
Bow: pernambuco with horsehair
Sound: bowing and sympathetic strings
First example: 1670

Cello

Voltaire was so enraptured
by the cellist Duport, he told
him he could work miracles,
and could turn a cow into a
'rossignol' or nightingale.

The cellist, Paul Tortelier playing a
very high note. His finger is
stopping the string near to the end
of the fingerboard, leaving only a
short length of string free to
vibrate.

Sometimes known as the violoncello, this instrument sounds
eight notes, an *octave*, deeper than the viola. Because of its
size it is too big to play 'under the chin', and so players hold it
between their knees. Originally they supported the whole
weight of the instrument with their legs, but now is it held on
a steel spike or *pin*.

Above: Cello with steel pin,
painted by Augustus John, 1923

Left: Cello of 1775 supported by
the player's knees

As well as stopping notes, the cellist, like other string players,
sometimes uses the left hand to produce *harmonics* by placing
a finger lightly on a string, but not pressing it on to the
fingerboard. If this is done, for example exactly halfway along
the string, both parts will vibrate, producing a clear, high
note known as a harmonic.

The cello has a strong smooth tone and has been used as a
solo instrument for several centuries. Bach wrote a series of
pieces for unaccompanied cello in which the technique of
double stopping is used. Two different notes are stopped at
once, and the bow drawn across the two strings
simultaneously so they sound together. *Triple stopping* is also
possible but the strings have to be bowed one after the other.

The cello makes up the fourth member of a string quartet. The other three are two violins ('first' and 'second') and a viola.

Profile
Size: 30 cm to 1.2 m
Made of: wood; gut strings and frets
Bow: pernambuco and hair
Sound made by: bowing
First example: 1470

Viol family

The viol family is made up of instruments which look quite like cellos of different sizes. But their tone is different: thinner and reedier. They have more strings (five or six) and frets, to help the player finger the notes correctly. The bow is slightly different too, and is held from below. They are often played in consorts, composed of viols of different sizes. A set of viols is called a 'chest of viols'.

Viols lost popularity to the violin family, but in the last few decades players have rediscovered how to play them, and much of the music written for them in earlier centuries.

Above: A gentleman of 1659 playing the viol

Right: A German family making up a consort of viols, painted in 1645

Double bass

A full-size symphony orchestra normally has eight double basses; sometimes more are required

Profile
Size: 1.9 m high
Made of: wood (mainly pine); ebony fingerboard, brass keys, steel or gut strings
Bow: 70 cm long, pernambuco wood, nylon or horsehair
Sound made by: bowing, plucking or slapping
First example of double bass instrument: 16th century

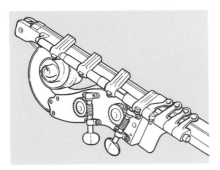

The double bass is the largest member of the string family. Because it is so big players have to stand, or sit on a high stool, to play it. The strings are so long and thick that machine heads are used in place of ordinary pegs. The picture opposite shows how these work.

The size of the instrument means that the fingers of the player's left hand have to stretch further to stop the different notes. The bow is held in the right hand in one of two ways.

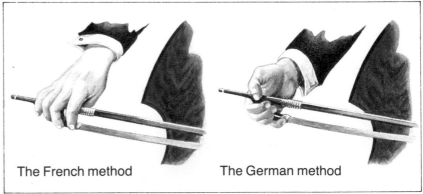

The French method   The German method

The right hand is also used for plucking the strings (*pizzicato*) and for other effects such as slapping the strings against the fingerboard. You can hear this in some jazz and dance bands.

Modern basses have either four or five strings. Five-string basses go down to C below the low E of the four-string bass, although some four-string instruments have an extension to lower the E string to C (left).

In 1713 an unwieldy double bass violin was nicknamed 'the monster'. Playing it was said to be 'fit only for a horse'.

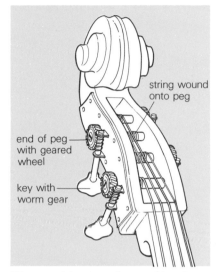

end of peg with geared wheel

key with worm gear

string wound onto peg

The machine heads used in place of pegs to hold the strings of a double bass in tune

The octobass, invented in 1849, was an experiment in making a double double bass. It had 3 strings, was 4.5 m high and was worked by levers and pedals.

Charles Mingus, the American jazz double bass player. As.well as being a virtuoso performer, he also wrote music for the different groups of musicians he worked with.

Double basses come in various shapes and sizes. Some look like large viols, with sloping shoulders, others look more like enormous violins. Sloping shoulders help a player reach the notes at the end of the fingerboard near the bridge. Since 1800 players have become better at performing on this huge, difficult instrument and composers have written tunes and pieces especially for it. There are over 200 concertos for the bass, but these are rarely performed. In a modern orchestra as many as ten double basses are used.

In ragtime, jazz and dance bands from the early 1900s, as well as folk groups, the double bass was first used to accompany other instruments or singers who played or sang the tune. In modern jazz, outstanding performers like Charles Mingus, Oscar Pettiford and Ray Brown have turned the double bass into a solo instrument with tunes of its own, either plucked or bowed.

As the double bass is big, heavy and awkward, it has always been difficult to carry around. The wooden case used to protect it, since it is delicate despite its size, can weigh more than the instrument itself! People used to put wheels on their cases to make getting about easier. Modern fibreglass cases are much lighter but a large car or van is still needed to move a bass easily. When an orchestra travels from city to city, half the pantechnicon may be filled with the double basses alone.

Guitar

Profile
Size: 1 m
Made of: wood: maple, ash, cherry; inlaid with rosewood; metal machine heads; steel, gut, or nylon strings
Plectrum: ivory, wood or metal
Sound made by: plucking or strumming with fingers or plectrum

Parts of modern Spanish guitar
1 nut; **2** fret; **3** fan struts; **4** table;
5 head; **6** neck; **7** heel; **8** foot;
9 back
The alternative dovetail method of construction **10** dovetail; **11** heel;
12 top block

The true origins of the guitar are unknown, but it may have developed from instruments used 3000 years ago in Asia. Or the instrument might have originated in Europe. There are many pictures of guitar-like instruments, some over 1000 years old, in European museums. The guitar as we know it today is a relatively new instrument, based on the designs of a Spaniard, Antonio de Torres.

The exploded diagram below shows how a modern Spanish guitar is made.

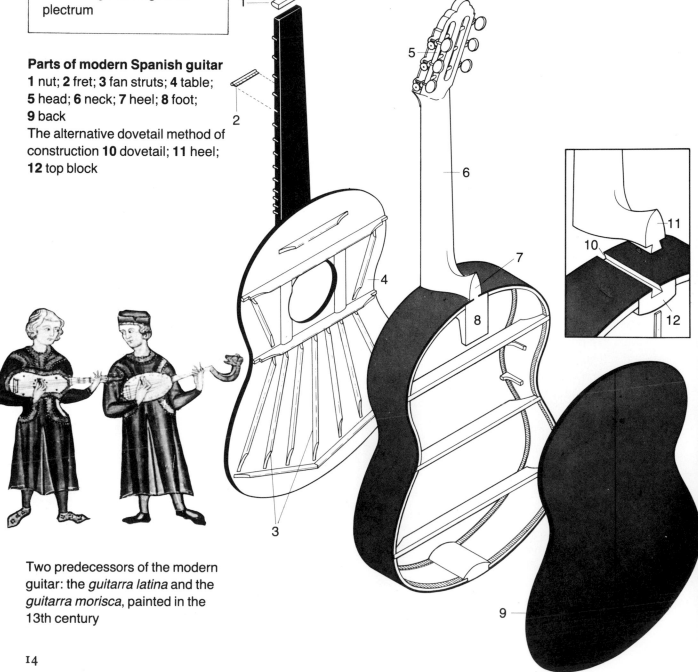

Two predecessors of the modern guitar: the *guitarra latina* and the *guitarra morisca*, painted in the 13th century

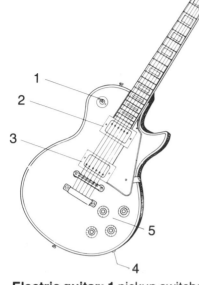

Electric guitar: 1 pickup switch;
2 bass and **3** treble pickups;
4 jack socket; **5** tone and volume
controls

There are six strings on most modern guitars and they are played by plucking the strings with fingers or a plectrum – a small thin piece of ivory, wood or metal. It is possible to play a tune with one note at a time or to play a chord by pulling the fingers of the right hand across several strings at once in one quick movement. This is called *strumming*, and accompanies all types of songs. As with the violin family the left hand changes the notes, but a guitar has *frets* – ridges across the neck of the instrument – and the notes are changed by moving the fingers and placing them behind the frets to *stop* the strings.

The acoustic or Spanish guitar is like a hollow box, and is up to 15 cm deep. The hole behind the strings and the empty space beneath amplify the sound. The electric guitar however has a thinner, or even solid, body and uses an amplifier to magnify the very quiet notes of the instrument, as with little or no resonating box the instrument does not amplify its own sound.

Three types of guitar. Above: Andrés Segovia playing a classical guitar; top right: Django Reinhardt playing a metal-string acoustic guitar; bottom right: The Pretenders playing electric guitars

Lute

Above: French lute tablature of 1728

The lute is a close relation of the guitar. It has Persian-Arabic origins, and this beautiful half-pear shaped instrument was probably brought to Western Europe by people returning from the Great Crusades. It was a fine court instrument of the fifteenth and sixteenth centuries, but it was difficult to make and perhaps even more difficult to play.

Lutes have a varying number of pairs of strings, tuned to the same note, called *courses*. Some instruments have as many as thirteen such courses – twenty-six strings in all – and in 1713 a musician named Mattheson pointed out that a lutenist spent most of the time tuning the instrument, rather than playing it.

The way in which lute music is written down is very different from that of other instruments. Instead of showing the *pitch* of a note, *tablature*, as it is called, shows by numbers and letters the different frets on which the fingers have to be placed to make the notes. It is almost a picture of the instrument's strings. A modern version of this kind of notation is used to indicate chords in some books of pieces for the guitar.

Below: woman playing the lute from a book of tablature

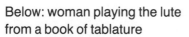

nuts
tuning pegs
frets
fingerboard
pegbox
soundhole
bridge
strings
soundboard
body
ribs

The Western lute

Mandolin

The mandolin is a smaller form of the lute, and it is played with a plectrum of tortoiseshell, whalebone, horn or ostrich quill. The word mandolin comes from an Italian word meaning almond, because of its shape. In fact, the shape of the mandolin was such that even the shell of a tortoise was once used to make the instrument.

The mandolin has a quiet, delicate tone and was mainly used as a solo instrument in the seventeenth century. It was not heard in England until 1713 'being an Instrument admired in Rome, but never Publick here'. In the last hundred years several orchestral parts have been written for it.

Banjo

Although the instrument is associated with popular music in America, banjos in Britain go back even further and probably originate from the lute and guitar. The main difference is that the banjo is made of a metal hoop with a membrane of vellum or plastic stretched over it like a drum head. Four or five strings lie over a movable bridge which stands on the vellum. The strings are plucked and the sound is different from that of a lute or guitar. A wooden resonator is fixed behind the hoop to make a 'back' for the instrument and amplify the sound. The banjo is now a common instrument, played all over the world.

Sitar

Indian sitar player Ravi Shankar. His concerts in Europe and America have led to a growing awareness of Indian music.

In India there is a family of stringed instruments which at first sight look like lutes. Many have a mixture of strings: those which are plucked and those which vibrate when others are played; these are called sympathetic strings. Indian music sounds quite different from much of Western music because the scale on which it is based does not have the same number of notes and has different sized intervals between them.

The sitar is the most popular instrument of Northern India. It has seven tuned strings of which two are *drone* strings. The player can move the frets, which are made of nylon or gut. Thirteen sympathetic strings vibrate when the main strings are played. A wire plectrum or long fingernails are used to play the sitar.

As well as its use in Indian music, the sitar has been used in Western popular music, and has been experimented with by rock groups including the Beatles.

Other plucked instruments

The vīnā has 7 strings and is plucked by fingernails grown specially long for the purpose.

Above: Unlike the vīnā which has a built-in resonator, the bīn has two gourds attached to the neck.
Right: The Pakistani rabāb is plucked with a wooden plectrum. It is popular in Afghanistan.

Hurdy-gurdy

This curious instrument, whose name comes from the continuous sound the instrument makes, is partly like a lute, partly like a guitar and partly like a bowed string instrument. It has no place in modern orchestral or popular music though.

The sound is made by the player turning a wheel, and like a violin bow, this sets the strings vibrating. The player's other hand presses down keys which stop the strings and change the notes. The tune which results has both a background drone and single played notes on top.

The hurdy-gurdy was popular in Europe during the middle ages and was used for religious music as well as for non-religious music. But it became a purely folk instrument and was played by wandering minstrels as an accompaniment to dancing on festival days. During the eighteenth century it was adopted by the French aristocracy as part of their fashionable interest in everything rustic, and Haydn and Mozart even wrote pieces for it.

Today it is still played in parts of Europe such as Hungary where it is known as the *tekero*. It is used either as a solo instrument or to accompany the clarinet and is played by gypsy musicians.

A hurdy-gurdy from a 14th-century psalter

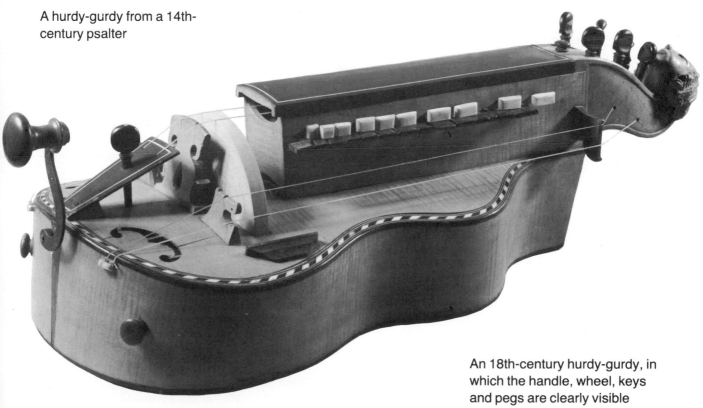

An 18th-century hurdy-gurdy, in which the handle, wheel, keys and pegs are clearly visible

Harp

Profile
Size: 1.8 m high
Weight: 35 kg
Made of: sycamore; deal
soundboard, nylon or steel
strings
Sound made by: plucking
First example:
Mesopotamia, 2500 BC

The harp is a very old instrument, probably originating over 4000 years ago. It may have first come from the eastern Mediterranean, from Egypt, Syria, Greece or Persia and from there it spread to Medieval Europe. The shape of the harp has not changed much in all those years. Several strings are stretched from a soundbox to the neck. Modern harps have up to 47 strings, grouped in different colours to help the player identify them. The soundbox amplifies the notes in the same way as the body of a violin or guitar. The notes are plucked by the player using both hands like this:

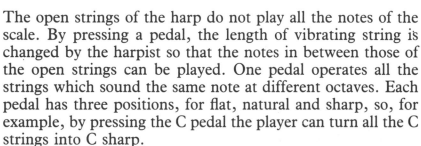

The open strings of the harp do not play all the notes of the scale. By pressing a pedal, the length of vibrating string is changed by the harpist so that the notes in between those of the open strings can be played. One pedal operates all the strings which sound the same note at different octaves. Each pedal has three positions, for flat, natural and sharp, so, for example, by pressing the C pedal the player can turn all the C strings into C sharp.

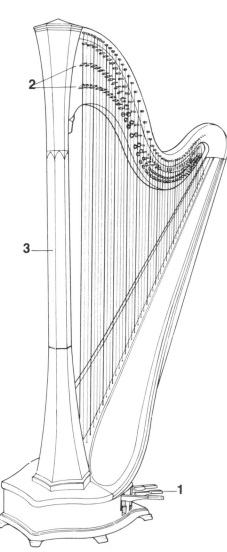

Left: Modern double-action harp.
There is a connection between the
pedals (**1**) and the discs (**2**) ,
running through the forepillar (**3**),
to alter the pitch of the strings.

Right: A medieval painting of King
David tuning a frame harp

Lyre

The lyre, like the harp, was first used by people living many thousands of years ago. The Greek poet Homer mentioned it frequently and the instrument has survived in many different forms to the present day. It can be found in Ethiopia and Uganda, where a wooden soundbox is covered with a soundboard of hide and has wooden arms supporting a yoke round which the strings are secured. It is played with a leather claw plectrum.

A modern concert harp showing pedals

Zither

The zither is another ancient instrument which is now played in many different parts of the world. The Middle Eastern variety consists of a shallow box over which metal and gut strings are stretched. The player uses a plectrum to play the tune on some strings, while plucking a series of open strings as an accompaniment. This is only one type however and there are trough zithers in Burundi, Korean long zithers and the Japanese half-tube zither.

An Ethiopian beganna, or box lyre

A board zither from the Middle East, known as a qānūn

The kinnor, a kind of lyre, was the national instrument of the ancient Jews. When David played before Saul, he used a kinnor – although the English version reads: 'When the evil spirit from God was upon Saul, David took an harp, and played with his hand'.

String terms

amplify: to make a sound louder. This can be done either by increasing the effect and level of sound of the vibrating string with a *soundboard* or electronically, by transmitting the sound through an amplifier.

body: part of a string instrument over which the strings are stretched

bow: length of wood with horsehair stretched between the ends

bridge: piece of carved balsa wood over which the strings lie. It carries the sound from the vibrating strings to the *soundboard*.

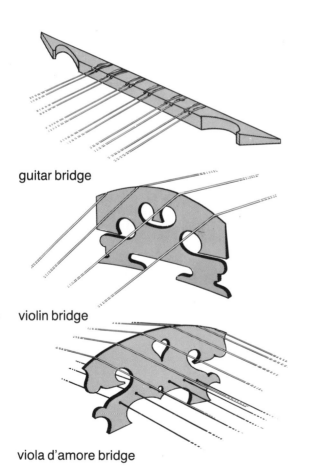

guitar bridge

violin bridge

viola d'amore bridge

capo: clip which can be fixed behind a guitar fret, crossing all the strings and shortening the length free to vibrate. All the strings then sound higher by the same degree.

chin rest: ebony, ivory or plastic shallow mould to help the player of a violin or viola to grip the instrument between chin and shoulder

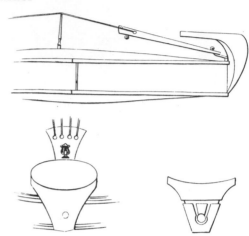

courses: pairs of strings tuned to the same pitch

double stopping: stopping two strings at once so that two pitches can sound together

drone: string which sounds continuously on the same note while an instrument is being played

fingerboard: part of string instrument on which the player's fingers are placed to stop the note

frets: pieces of gut or metal stretched across the fingerboard. The player's fingers are placed behind the fret to stop the note.

frog: device for tightening the hair of a bow

harmonic: by lightly stopping a string at a point which is a fraction of its total length, such as a half or a quarter, a pure sound can be produced which is higher in pitch than if the string were fully stopped

keys or pegs: these are used to tighten strings and keep them in tune. Fine adjusters are also on the *tailpieces* of violins, violas and cellos.

mute: clip made of ivory or metal fixed on the bridge to muffle or alter the sound

frets

open string: string free to vibrate over its total length

pickup: electronic device which transmits the sound of the instrument to an *amplifier*

pizzicato: using the fingers or fingernails to pluck the string and make it vibrate

plectrum: piece of plastic, ivory, metal, shell or horn used to pluck the strings of guitars, banjos and similar instruments

principal: senior member of each section in an orchestra

resonate: vibrate sympathetically

rosin or *resin:* sap from pine trees solidified and spread on the hair of a bow to make it sticky and grip the string

soundbox: the *body* of a string instrument consisting of a hollow wooden box which *resonates* when the strings are played, thus amplifying the sound

soundhole: opening in the *soundbox* which increases the volume of the instrument

soundpost: piece of wood holding the two sides of the *soundbox* apart and transmitting the vibrations from one side to the other

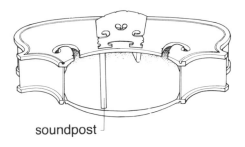

soundpost

stopping: pressing the fingers on to the strings of an instrument to shorten them and change the pitch of the note

strumming: plucking several strings together (usually on the guitar) in a regular rhythm

sympathetic strings: strings which vibrate when other strings on the same instrument are plucked or bowed

tailpiece: wood or metal device at lower end of string instrument to which the strings are attached

triple stopping: stopping three strings at the same time

vellum: parchment-like skin on a banjo, used to amplify the sound of the vibrating strings

Here are some of the settings in which string instruments can be heard today.

One of the world's most famous string quartets is the Amadeus, which was founded in 1947

Jazz violinist Stephane Grappelli, who has shown how jazz can be played successfully on this instrument

The classical Indian singer Mohammal Ismail photographed in Jaipur accompanying himself on the tampura or long-necked Indian lute

Woodwind *Some instruments in use today*

Between them, the members of the woodwind family make more different sounds than any other family of instruments. One clue to the reason why lies in the great variety of shapes and sizes you can see in the picture above.

Woodwind instruments are not always made of wood. They are also made from metals like brass, silver, gold and platinum, and a whole range of other materials, including ebony, horn, ivory, bone and plastics.

The noise made by a wind instrument comes from the air inside its *pipe* vibrating regularly. The vibrations are picked up by the ears of the listener, whose eardrums vibrate, sending electrical impulses, which create the sensation of sound, to the brain.

1 descant recorder
2 piccolo
3 flute
4 alto flute
5 bass flute
6 E♭ clarinet
7 clarinet
8 bass clarinet
9 double bass clarinet
10 soprano saxophone
11 alto saxophone
12 tenor saxophone
13 baritone saxophone
14 oboe
15 cor anglais
16 bassoon
17 double bassoon
18 accordion
19 highland bagpipes

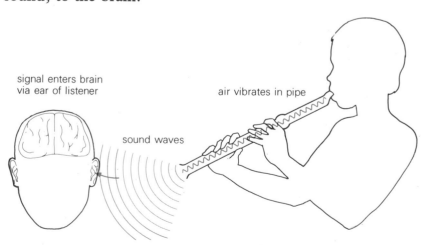

signal enters brain
via ear of listener

air vibrates in pipe

sound waves

How is the sound made?

What makes the air column vibrate?
Woodwind instruments are divided into groups according to the way their *air column* is made to vibrate.

Edge-tone

1 Vertically-blown
Panpipes
2 Flue-blown (duct flutes)
Primitive whistles, gemshorn, pitchpipe, swanee whistle, instruments such as number 1 in the illustration on the previous page
3 Transversely-blown (transverse flutes)
Instruments numbered 2 to 5

Reed

1 Single-reed
Instruments numbered 6 to 13 along with some more primitive instruments like the chalumeau
2 Double-reed
Shawms, curtalls, crumhorns, rackets, and instruments numbered 14 to 17
3 Free-reed
Instruments numbered 18 and 19
Bagpipes have both double-reed and single-reed methods of producing vibrations of the air column.

Now let us see in more detail how these various groups make their sounds.

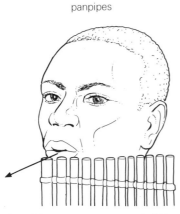

panpipes

player blows across open end of pipe

Edge-tone
1 In panpipes the player's breath is blown across the top of the pipe. It hits the opposite edge, splits, and sets the air in the pipe vibrating.

2 In flue-blown flutes, or duct flutes, a whistle *mouthpiece* makes a more efficient job of directing the player's breath at the *lip* which splits the air stream.

3 Transverse flutes work rather like panpipes, but the hole, or *embouchure*, blown across by the player is in the side of the pipe. The breath is therefore directed at the opposite edge of the embouchure.

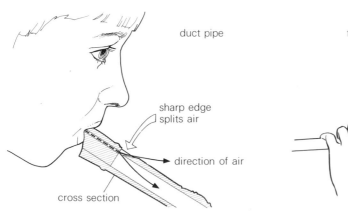

duct pipe

sharp edge splits air

direction of air

cross section

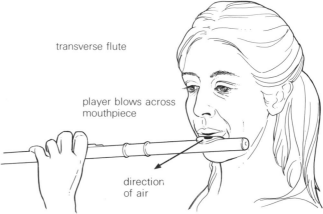

transverse flute

player blows across mouthpiece

direction of air

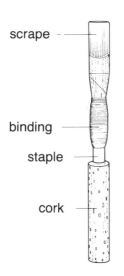

Double reed of an oboe

Reed

1 The single reed, fastened by a *ligature* to a mouthpiece held between the player's lips, beats (or vibrates) when the air stream hits it. This causes the air column in the pipe attached to the mouthpiece to vibrate.

2 The double reed is really one reed bent over, cut in two and tied firmly round a hollow *staple*. The reed is held between the player's lips and the air stream causes the two, paper-thin halves to vibrate regularly. The reed, blown on its own produces a harsh 'crowing' noise, but when this is transmitted through the staple to the instrument's tube it turns into the instrument's recognisable tone.

3 The free reed is metal and fastened at one end but free to vibrate otherwise. The air stream is directed at the reed under pressure and can only escape by way of the gap normally covered by the reed. As the reed beats, so the air column in the adjacent *resonator* vibrates and amplifies the sound.

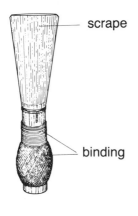

Double reed of a bassoon

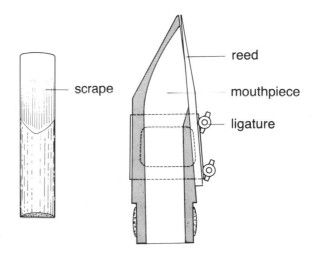

Single reed of a clarinet and a clarinet mouthpiece with the reed in position, held by a ligature

Although it is referred to as 'cane', the best reeds are made from a tall grass or reed called *arundo donax*. This grows in southern Europe, particularly around Fréjus on France's Mediterranean coast. Harvested when still unripe, it is left to mature in the open air.

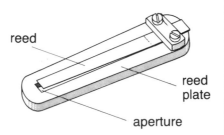

Free reed of a concertina

'Reed players are entirely dependent upon a short-lived vegetable matter of merciless capriciousness, with which ... when it behaves, are wrought ... the most tender and expressive sounds.'
Anthony Baines

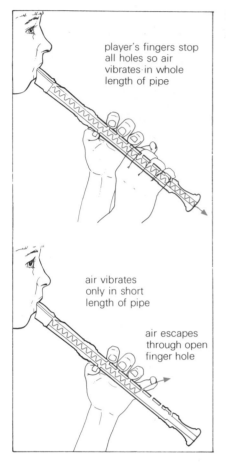

player's fingers stop all holes so air vibrates in whole length of pipe

air vibrates only in short length of pipe

air escapes through open finger hole

How does the player make different notes?

The shorter the column of vibrating air the higher the note, and the longer the vibrating air column, the lower the note. Different notes can be produced by the same pipe. This is achieved by boring holes in the pipe, which are covered usually by the player's fingers. Air always takes a short-cut, and if the player uncovers a hole the air will rush out. It then only vibrates in the shorter length of the pipe from reed or mouthpiece to the hole. This is basically the way the pitch of a note is controlled.

In order to produce the required notes, holes must often be bored in positions which are inconvenient for the fingers. To get over this difficulty, *keys* are used. These are levers with one end positioned conveniently for the finger, the other fastened to a metal flap which closes over the hole. To ensure air-tightness, the flap carries a pad made from leather, felt, plastic, or cork. By pressing the key the player lifts the pad from the hole. Keys are returned to their normal position after use by a metal spring.

Another element involved in changing the pitch of a note is the speed of the air travelling down the air column. Higher notes can be obtained by blowing harder into the pipe which speeds up the airflow. This is called *overblowing*. Often this is helped by opening an extra key called an *octave* or *register key*. This operates a small hole high on the pipe which shortens the vibrations within the whole instrument.

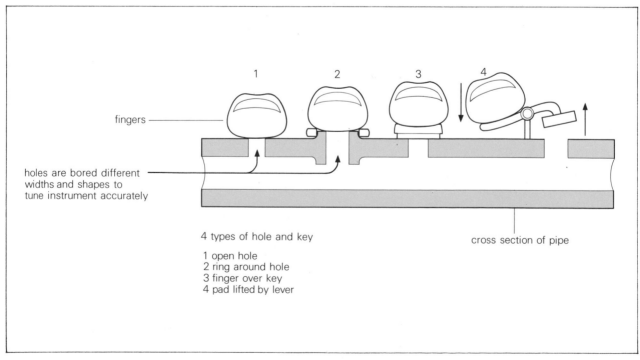

fingers

holes are bored different widths and shapes to tune instrument accurately

4 types of hole and key

1 open hole
2 ring around hole
3 finger over key
4 pad lifted by lever

cross section of pipe

Fill a narrow bottle and a wide bottle with water until you can blow the same note across their necks. What about the timbre?

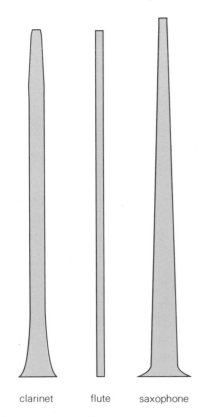

clarinet   flute   saxophone

Instrument profiles

Why do different instruments make different sounds?

The particular sound made by an instrument is called its tone quality or *timbre*. This is affected by several factors.

1 The method of generating the sound

As we have already seen, this might be by the player's breath hitting a sharp edge, or setting a single or double reed in vibration. In some free-reed instruments and bagpipes the wind is provided not by the player's breath but by *bellows* of various types.

2 The profile of the tube

The *profile* or shape of a section cut along the tube of the instrument is very important in its influence on the timbre, the tuning of the instrument and at what interval it overblows. Some instruments are cylindrical, the *bore* remaining almost the same from beginning to end (as in the clarinet). Others are quite conical, becoming wider from the end closest to the player to the *bell* (like the saxophone).

3 The material the instrument is made from

Scientists and musicians disagree about the influence of the material from which the instrument is made. Generally, experiments have shown that this makes little difference. However, all players feel that some materials help them to make a better sound than others, and there are strong feelings about this on the part of those who, for example, feel they can play better on a wooden flute than one made of gold, and vice versa.

4 The player

There is some evidence that the physical characteristics of the player affect the type of sound they make on their instrument. Obviously lung capacity could be important, but it may also be important to bear in mind the effect of the size of the mouth and even the skull!

These two pictures from the Yamaha instrument factory show the difference in shape between the flute (left) and the soprano saxophone (right). At this stage, before keys are fitted, the tone and finger-holes are made in the basic pipe.

Early woodwind instruments

Some of the ancestors of the woodwind family are now often revived by early music groups.

Although the ocarina was originally an ancient African instrument made from a coconut shell, its present shape comes from an Italian whistle made to look like a bird. The order in which the 10 holes are opened doesn't matter: each gives a higher note. In 1939 Bing Crosby was backed by a group of them in *When the Sweet-potato Piper plays*.

Set of four gemshorns

Gemshorn
Gemse, or *Gemsbock* are German names for the chamois, and it was from this animal's backward-pointing horns that these ancient instruments were made. Several *finger-holes* were bored in the side and the wide end was stopped with a wooden plug, leaving just enough room for the player's breath to enter. It was an early type of recorder, the air set in vibration by a *lip* in the wall of the instrument. The tone was very quiet.

Panpipes
The ancient Greeks told the story of the nymph Syrinx, chased into a reed bed by the god Pan. He made his first pipe from some of the reeds. *Syrinx* was the Greek name for panpipes, but instruments of this type were also played in China by 1100 BC. Today they can be found in many parts of the world. They consist of a number of pipes of different lengths each of which makes a separate note, bound together, or sometimes carved from a solid block. Debussy's *Syrinx* for unaccompanied concert flute imitates the panpipes' sound.

Ugandan panpipes. The player blows across the top of one pipe after another to make a tune.

Shawm, painted in the late 15th century

Above: Woman playing a crumhorn, painted in 1510
Right: Carving of a Renaissance racket

Shawm

A type of shawm was known in the East 5000 years ago. The player's lips rested on a circular lip-rest allowing the reed to vibrate freely. Its conical shape, combined with the broad double reed, gave a loud, clear sound suitable for military music. They were normally made in *treble*, *tenor* and *bass* sizes, although larger ones were known. In Europe it reached its peak during the fifteenth century. Introduced during the Islamic occupation of Spain, it remains in both the Basque region and Catalonia where a metal type called a *tenora* is still made.

Crumhorn

The crumhorn is played like the recorder, but the actual sound is made by a double reed inside the cap of the instrument. The tone is deep and quiet, like humming. It can make only about nine notes, although one or two keys can be added to give lower notes. The instrument originated in the medieval bladder-pipe, a bagpipe with an animal's bladder. Its name came from *crump* 'crooked', a description of its bent-up lower end. Sets, or consorts, of crumhorns appeared from about 1500 onwards. Henry VIII owned several. Owing to its restricted sound, few notes and general playing problems no modern instrument has derived from it.

Racket

Though only 30 cm tall the feeble-toned racket can play as low as the F one note above the deepest on the four-string double bass. Six or more narrow tubes, joined together, are bored inside it and the player blows a double reed and controls ten or twelve finger holes with the tips and joints of fingers and thumbs. It was heard in France and Germany between 1500 and 1700.

Thomas Stanesby, a London instrument maker, made a racket according to French instructions. 'But it did not answer expectation'; by reason of its closeness, the interior parts imbibed and retained the moisture of the breath, the ducts dilated and broke. In short the whole blew up.'

Recorders

The Dolmetsch Consort, all members of the Dolmetsch family, playing four different sizes of recorder: descant, treble, tenor and bass

Profile
Size: sopranino 24 cm, descant 34 cm, treble 45 cm, tenor 64 cm, bass 92 cm
Made of: wood, plastic
Sound made by: edge-tone
First example: England, 12th century
Relations: gemshorn, flageolet

The name recorder comes from the old English *record*, 'to sing like a bird'.
'The nymph did earnestly contest
whether the birds or she recorded best.'
Browne, *Britannia's Pastorals*.

Thousands of boys and girls now play recorders, and many composers write music for these attractively soft-toned instruments. Yet when your grandmother was a girl she had probably never heard or seen one, despite their having been invented hundreds of years earlier.

A recorder-type instrument, made from the tibia (thigh bone) of a roe deer, with three finger-holes, was found in a pre-Roman Iron Age jar in Jutland, and various instruments of this type were known in the early Middle Ages. But the instruments really developed during the fifteenth and sixteenth centuries. In the early 1500s there were often consorts of a treble, two tenors and a bass. Samuel Pepys heard recorders for the first time in a play in 1668. 'The wind-musick when the angel comes down was so sweet that it ravished me', he wrote in his diary. During the eighteenth century, with the new fashion for contrast between soft and loud playing, the recorder lost out to the *transverse* flute. Today, however, it is frequently heard, not only in the classroom but also in the concert hall, as more people become interested in hearing music played on the instruments for which it was actually written.

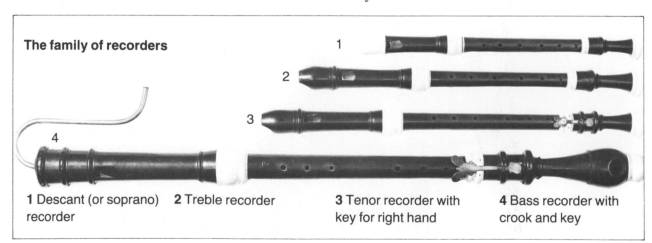

The family of recorders

1 Descant (or soprano) recorder **2** Treble recorder **3** Tenor recorder with key for right hand **4** Bass recorder with crook and key

A Dolmetsch recorder being hand turned

Recorders generally have seven finger-holes and one for the thumb and are played with a whistle-type mouthpiece. The tenor and bass have a key covering the lowest hole. The bass also has a metal crook so the player can hold it more comfortably. Recorders were made from wood but for the past 40 years plastic has often been used.

The revival of the recorder early in the twentieth century was due entirely to one man, Arnold Dolmetsch. He was one of the few people to own a recorder but in 1919 he left it on a railway station platform and had to make a replacement. After several attempts he produced a successful instrument which he later went on to manufacture commercially. The story's happy end came when his original recorder was bought by a friend of his for 5 shillings (25p) from a junk shop near the station!

Pipe and tabor

These are two different instruments played simultaneously by the same player. The pipe is a short *duct flute* with three holes. It is played and supported with the left hand, and by overblowing to make higher notes a simple dance tune can be played. At the same time the player's right hand beats the tabor, a small drum with a gut snare. This effective and economical accompaniment has a long history. A pipe and tabor player is shown in the *Cantigas di S Maria* from about 1270.

Flageolet

The flageolet has four finger-holes on the top and two on the underside. The ivory mouthpiece fits into the pear-shaped top of the instrument which contains a sponge to absorb the moisture of the breath. It was first heard in 1581, was ousted by the recorder in seventeenth-century England, and fitted with keys in the nineteenth century to become a member of fashionable quadrille bands. Double flageolets, with two tubes giving two notes at the same time, were quite common.

The earliest known single-note whistles date from 10,000 BC, made from reindeer bones

Left: A Spanish pipe and tabor player
Right: Double flageolet made in about 1830 (left); French flageolet of around 1850 (middle); 19th-century English flageolet (right)

Flute

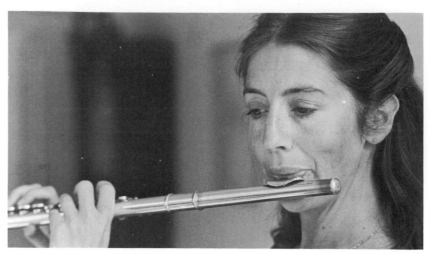

A fife player, painted by Edouard Manet in 1866

In 1774 the Gentlemen's Concerts were begun in Manchester by 26 amateur musicians. Since they all played the flute, for some years the orchestra consisted exclusively of 26 flautists.

The flute has a wide range of tone and pitch. This is the main reason it displaced the recorder. Its lowest notes are rich and beautiful; the medium range pure and limpid; higher notes brilliant and full. The flute is also the most agile of all the wind instruments.

Until the nineteenth century the holes were always bored at equal distances from each other, making it difficult for flutes to be played in tune. A key was added to help, and by 1820 eight keys had become usual. But this was still not satisfactory and in the nineteenth century Theobald Boehm (who was trained both as a musician and a jeweller) devised a new type of flute with a more efficient system of keys. This was completed by 1847 and, with a few modifications, is still in use today.

The flute is made in three sections: *head joint*, with the *embouchure* and *plug; middle joint*, and *foot joint*, carrying the Boehm-system *keywork* and *side-holes*. The range of the flute is about three octaves, the player producing the second and third octaves by narrowing the flow of air into the flute.

The different voices of the flute are heard in Debussy's *L'après-midi d'un faune*, Gluck's 'Dance of the Blessed Spirits' from *Orfeo*, and Rossini's *William Tell* overture. Flutes are found in all sorts of wind bands, and there are famous jazz players like Herbie Mann. Often in jazz and rock bands the flute is amplified.

Fife

Used for military purposes as long ago as the Middle Ages, this was probably the first of the small transverse flutes playing an octave higher than normal. Some regiments still have drum and fife bands and until the end of the last century there were official fife calls, sounded to drum accompaniment.

Profile
Size: 30 cm long
Made of: wood, silver, alloys
Sound made by: edge-tone
First example: late 18th
century
Relations: flute, fife

Piccolo

Bass flute

Concert
flute

Alto flute

Piccolo

The Italians called this half-size flute *flauto piccolo*, 'little flute'. It came into use towards the end of the eighteenth century, playing notes an octave higher than the normal flute. The modern piccolo has Boehm-system keywork and in a symphony orchestra it is usually played by the third flautist, who 'doubles' – that is, plays either piccolo or third flute as required.

The lowest notes are very weak, but as they get higher they get stronger, and the shrill highest notes of all can be heard above the largest orchestra. Beethoven used a piccolo in his Fifth Symphony, and there are solos in Tchaikovsky's Fourth Symphony and the 'Farandole' from Bizet's *L'Arlésienne*. It is a regular member of wind bands, where it is heard to perfection in the remarkable solo in Sousa's march *The Stars and Stripes Forever*.

Alto flute

This large flute, which plays four notes lower than the normal flute, is sometimes mistakenly called the bass flute. It was perfected by Boehm, tends to play sad music, and was used effectively by Ravel in *Daphnis and Chloé*.

Bass flute

The true bass flute is a twentieth-century invention, playing an octave lower than the ordinary flute. The tube is so long that it is bent into a U-shape so that it can be held and played like other flutes. The first was made by the Italian Abelardo Albisi and opera composers like Mascagni and Puccini were the first to use it. It is often heard in film and television background music and several jazz flautists – notably Roland Kirk – have specialised in bass flute.

Because the tubes of the alto and bass flutes are so long they would be too heavy if made from wood. The alto is therefore made of silver, the bass of a silver-plated alloy.

Right: Eric Dolphy was one of the first modern jazz players to use the flute. He also played saxophone and bass clarinet.

Clarinet

Right: Players of E♭, B♭ and bass
clarinet all fingering C
Far right: Fingering chart showing
covered ● and open ○ holes
playing written middle C

Profile
Size: B♭ 66 cm long
Made of: wood, ebonite,
plastic, metal (less often)
Sound made by: single reed
First example: Germany
about 1700
Relations: chalumeau

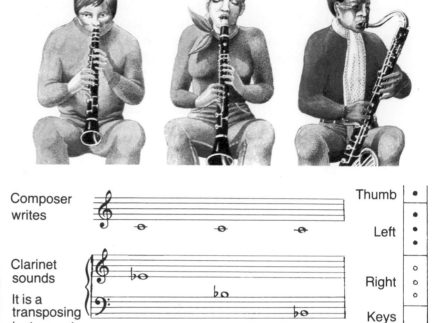

Composer writes

Clarinet sounds

It is a transposing instrument

Thumb	●
Left	● ● ●
Right	○ ○ ○
Keys	

The index finger and thumb of
jazzman Kenny Davern's left hand
show how the player changes
register from upper to lower with
the holes and keys at the top of
the instrument.

The clarinet *overblows* twelve notes higher, not an octave like the flute. This made fingering very complicated on early clarinets. Music with many sharps or flats led to even more complications. To help overcome these, in addition to the clarinet in C (that is, one which sounds C when C is fingered), a clarinet in B flat (which sounds the note B flat when C is fingered) and one in A (the fingering for C producing the note A) were made. These lower clarinets, being longer, have more attractive tones, so the clarinet in C is now a rare instrument.

Instruments of the clarinet type played with a single reed were known to very early civilisations. A double clarinet is shown on a relief from 2700 BC in a Cairo museum. Later, came the French *chalumeau*, a cane forming the tube and the reed cut from the tube or tied on. At the end of the seventeenth century, Johann Christian Denner of Nuremberg made an instrument of this type with two keys, but the name clarinet was not seen until about 1732.

Since 1844 developments in the fingering system by Boehm, Muller and Albert have helped to make the clarinet one of the most versatile instruments in the orchestra, with a range of forty-five notes. It is very agile and as effective playing slow melodies as leaping from note to note. Two were included in most orchestras by the end of the eighteenth century. Orchestral players have both a B flat and an A clarinet, playing each as appropriate.

Eb   Bb   Alto Basset horn

Bass   Double bass

You can hear the clarinet in Rimsky-Korsakov's *Sheherazade*, Weber's *Oberon* overture and the upwards *glissando* (slide through the notes) at the opening of Gershwin's *Rhapsody in Blue*. Wind bands have several, a clarinet appears in a traditional jazz band, and big band saxophone players double on clarinet.

E flat clarinet

This is the only high clarinet still in use. It was invented about 1800 and plays four notes higher than the B flat clarinet. Its grotesque, cheeky sound is heard in the 'Witches Sabbath' from Berlioz's *Symphonie Fantastique* and Strauss illustrated many of *Till Eulenspiegel's* merry pranks with it. It is also used in wind bands.

Alto clarinet

This was invented in 1792. It could play three notes lower than the B flat clarinet, but the modern version can play four or five notes lower.

Basset horn

An *alto* clarinet with a narrow bore was first made by Mayrhofer of Passau in 1770. Originally it was crescent-shaped but by 1800 was almost bent into a right-angle. It was straightened out later in the century by Grenser of Dresden. This soft-toned, sombre instrument was a great favourite of Mozart's. He used it in twenty works, including the opera *The Magic Flute* and his *Requiem*. In 1909 Strauss wrote for it in *Elektra*.

Bass clarinet

The low, oily sounds of the bass clarinet were first heard after Sax invented the modern version in 1836, although isolated and often bizarre types had been made since 1772. The present-day model looks like a wooden saxophone with an upturned metal *bell*, and rests on a spike when being played. Materials, keywork and mouthpiece are like those of the clarinet, but bigger. It is heard in bands (Sousa had two) and in the orchestra, especially in Tchaikovsky's *Nutcracker* and César Franck's Symphony.

Double bass clarinet

In 1890 Fontaine-Besson made a giant clarinet an octave deeper than the bass clarinet. Usually made of metal with Boehm system keywork, by bending the tube it stands no more than 200 cm high. Schoenberg used one in his *Five orchestral pieces* and it is found in large wind bands.

Saxophones

The London Saxophone Quartet

Profile
Size: soprano 68 cm; alto
68 cm; tenor 83 cm; baritone
98 cm; bass 113 cm
Made of: brass, plastic
Sound made by: single reed
First example: France 1846
Relations: clarinets

The Belgian instrument maker and inventor Adolphe Sax (1814-1894) created several families of instruments, including saxhorns, saxtrombas and saxtubas, but his name is mainly associated with the saxophones.

There were fourteen different sizes when the family was completed in 1846, from sopranino to contrabass. Five of these, soprano, alto, tenor, baritone and bass, remain in use. Each plays four or five notes lower than the one above. Saxophones have a single reed, like a clarinet; their tube is very conical and made from brass (or often plastic); and the fingering system is a cross between that of the oboe and Boehm system.

The soprano is usually (though not always) made straight, looking like a metal clarinet, and the others are doubled back on themselves. These all hang from the player's neck by a sling so that the fingers are free to deal with the keys.

Soon after their invention, saxophones were adopted by French army bands and since they are *transposing instruments*, use the same system of written music as recorders and clarinets. The fingering remains constant in relation to the written notes, but the pitch that results varies according to the size and key of the instrument.

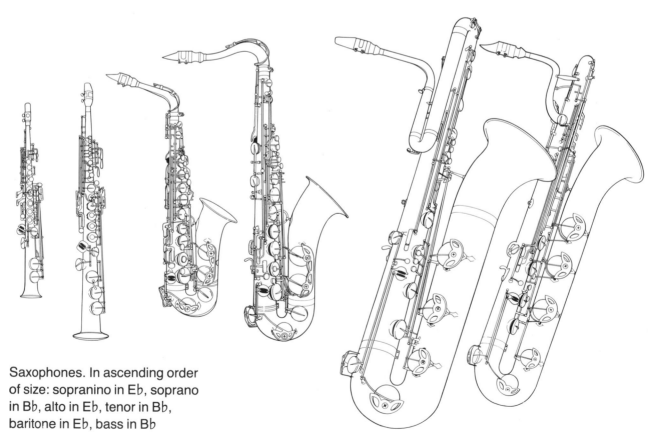

Saxophones. In ascending order of size: sopranino in E♭, soprano in B♭, alto in E♭, tenor in B♭, baritone in E♭, bass in B♭

Charlie Parker (alto) was the first important modern jazz saxophone soloist.

Coleman Hawkins (tenor) was a great soloist in all periods of jazz from swing to modern.

Sidney Bechet was the most famous soprano saxophone player in early or traditional jazz. Born in New Orleans, he later settled in France.

Saxophones can normally produce about 33 notes, but in the 1920s the Argentinian Texiero de Ladario used a special type to play up to 48.

The Tarogato was an ancient Hungarian instrument, a wide-bore oboe used in military music. In 1900 W J Schunda of Budapest fitted it with a saxophone mouthpiece. You may hear it played today.

Alto, tenor and baritone saxophones are found in army bands in many countries, and various sizes of saxophones are sometimes invited into the orchestra, usually to play a solo part. Bizet asked for an alto in *L'Arlésienne;* Ravel needed soprano, alto and tenor saxophones in *Bolero* and alto in *Pictures from an Exhibition.* Walton, Britten and Vaughan Williams have all specified saxophones. Debussy wrote a *Rhapsodie* and Ibert a concerto for alto saxophone with orchestra.

The saxophones have proved most useful in the world of jazz and popular music. Outstanding jazz players include Sidney Bechet and John Coltrane (soprano); Paul Desmond, Johnny Hodges and Charlie Parker (alto); Coleman Hawkins, Stan Getz, and Lester Young (tenor); Harry Carney and Gerry Mulligan (baritone); and Adrian Rollini (bass). Between them, these distinguished performers cover the whole of jazz history and every style. The saxophone is also important in many rock bands.

In the dance band of the 1920s saxophones were often played by musicians who doubled on the violin or cello for sweeter music. By the 1940s the normal dance band included two altos, two tenors and a baritone. With players doubling on various clarinets, flutes or oboe, this has remained the basic big band and stage band reed section.

Oboe

The oboist's *embouchure*, demonstrated by Heinz Holliger

'Oboe' is derived from the French name for the shawm, *Hautbois*, or 'loud woodwind'.

If you have ever heard an orchestra tuning up you will know that just before the concert is due to begin, the *sub-leader* stands and turns to the first oboe who plays a single long note. This is an A, produced by air vibrating about 440 times a second. Orchestras all over the world tune to A, although the exact frequency can vary from country to country between 440 and 443.

The oboe is chosen to play the note because from the time it became the first regular wind-instrument member of the orchestra, in the late seventeenth century, its stable pitch made it a reliable companion.

The oboe has a distinctive, 'reedy' sound. Its ancestor was the shawm, but while the double reed of the shawm was completely free to vibrate as the player's lips rested on the *pirouette*, the reed of the oboe is gripped between the lips and is thus under much more control.

Early oboes had seven holes and one key, as the lowest hole was too far away for the player's finger to be able to cover it. In the course of time more holes and keys were added, and the modern oboe has an elaborate key mechanism with two octave keys.

The wistful sounds of the oboe, which is agile as well as soulful, can be heard in the opening of the second movement of Brahms's Violin Concerto, in Schubert's Ninth Symphony, and in Rossini's *Silken Ladder* overture. It is found also in wind bands, but not often in jazz, although the American Bob Cooper and English Karl Jenkins have shown its possibilities.

Oboe d'amore

The larger oboe d'amore plays three notes below the normal oboe. It was probably invented in Germany around 1720. The tone is beautiful and warm. J S Bach asked for the oboe d'amore in no fewer than forty-nine cantatas and two settings of the Passion. Two are used with contralto voice in 'Ah, Golgotha' from the *St Matthew Passion*.

Cor anglais

At the beginning of the eighteenth century a larger type of oboe, playing lower notes, was called an *oboe da caccia*. By the end of the century a pear-shaped bell had been fitted, softening the sound. When made in curved form the instrument was named the cor anglais. This may have been because the instrument looked like a type of English hunting horn (*cor anglais* means 'English horn'), or perhaps the name was originally *cor anglé* (meaning 'angled horn'). The instrument, straightened out in 1839, and now known as the English horn can be heard in Berlioz' *Symphonie Fantastique*.

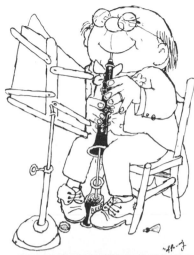

Bass oboe

The first bass oboe, sounding a whole octave deeper than the normal oboe, was made by Denner about 1700. From time to time over the next 200 years specimens were built, but it did not attract composers, although in 1914 Holst used it in his suite *The Planets* which requires an extremely large orchestra.

Heckelphone

In 1904 William Heckel invented this double-reed instrument covering much the same range of notes as the bass oboe. It has a globular bell and seems more satisfactory generally. Richard Strauss wrote a part for it in his *Salomé* the year after its invention.

Above: The oboe section of the BBC Symphony Orchestra with the cor anglais in the foreground

Left: Adjusting the reed of an oboe

Bassoon

Bassoon   Double bassoon

'The wedding guest
   here beat his breast
For he heard the loud
   bassoon.'
Coleridge, *The Rime of the Ancient Mariner*

In the late sixteenth century double-reed bass instruments appeared, with a tube of such length that it was doubled back on itself to be easily manageable. Originally the two tubes were bored in the same block of wood, and such instruments were known as dulcians. Since the seventeenth century the two tubes have been inserted separately into the *butt* which joins them. One tube, the long joint, finishes in a small bell; the other, the wing joint, has a brass or silver *crook* inserted into its top and this carries the double reed. This instrument is generally known as the bassoon, although early versions were called curtalls.

In the early days there were five sizes of bassoon, ranging from 38 cm to 144 cm in height. The modern instrument is definitely a bass instrument, with a tube 253 cm in total length and a range of notes from just below the deepest on the cello to about the highest of the horn. It can thus also cope with tenor parts, when necessary.

Although the bassoon was one of the earliest woodwind instruments in the orchestra, and in the eighteenth century was a popular soloist, in 1885 the musicologist Gevaert wrote: 'It is satisfied to be a tireless servant in the orchestra: of all the wind instruments it is the one that has the least rest'.

In the orchestra it often plays the bass part along with the cellos, and frequently helps to fill in the harmony with clarinets and horns. But concertos have been written for bassoon. (Mozart, who wrote concertos for all the woodwind, wrote a very popular one.) The lower notes of the bassoon are serious and grave, yet it's also a very nimble instrument and these two contrary characteristics sometimes make it sound very humorous. In Prokofiev's *Peter and the Wolf* it plays the part of the grandfather. There is a yearning solo for bassoon in the opening of Tchaikovsky's Sixth Symphony, and another using the highest notes begins Stravinsky's *Rite of Spring*.

Double bassoon

The Waits' Band at Exeter in 1575 included a double curtall. About 1618 the double bassoon was first heard, its double-length tube producing sounds an octave lower than the ordinary bassoon. It remained a band instrument until Haydn used it in his oratorio *The Creation* in 1798. Here its low, writhing notes painted a picture in sound of the moment when 'creeps, with sinuous trace, the worm'. Beethoven used the double bassoon in his Fifth and Ninth Symphonies and it became a regular member of the orchestra (played by a member doubling on the bassoon) shortly afterwards. Ravel's *Mother Goose* and Dukas's *Sorcerer's Apprentice* along with Berg's *Wozzeck* show that the double bassoon is as agile as the ordinary bassoon.

The rare metal double bassoon has all its holes covered by keys, but the normal wooden type is controlled by any of the ordinary bassoon fingering systems. It can be as high as 254 cm if made in bassoon shape with one fold, but giving the tube an extra fold reduces the height; four folds result in an instrument about 142 cm tall.

Profile

Size:142 cm to 254 cm tall

Made of: wood, metal (rare)

Sound made by: double reed

First example: early 17th century

Relations: oboes, bassoon

Baritone sarrusophone in E♭ made in the late 19th century

Above: Bassoon maker of the 17th century, at work
Left: Dulcian player in a picture of the mid 17th century

Sarrusophone

In 1856 a French bandmaster named Sarrus patented the Sarrusophones, six sizes of brass instruments with conical profiles played with double reeds. He hoped they would replace the military band oboes and bassoons, but only the contrabass had any success. It plays roughly the same notes as the double bassoon; several composers have used it, including Saint-Saëns and Massenet. The English composer Delius included one in his *Eventyr*.

Free-reed instruments

Right: Diagram of an accordion showing its working parts. **1** treble keyboard; **2** treble reed block; **3** bass keyboard mechanism; **4** bass keyboard; **5** bass reed blocks

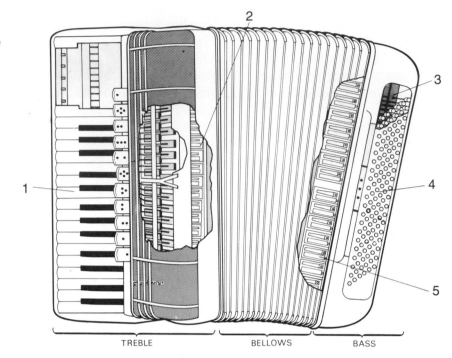

TREBLE   BELLOWS   BASS

Below: diagram of a concertina with one casing raised to show its working parts. **1** reed plate; **2** leather valve; **3** free reed; **4** reed cavity

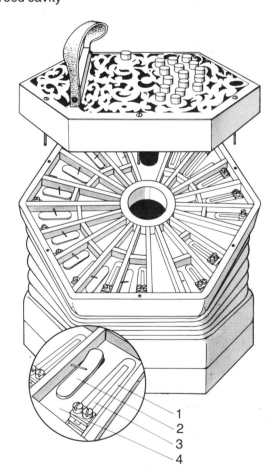

Accordion
The first European accordion was patented by by C F L Buschmann in 1821–2. But similar instruments existed in China and Japan as early as 1100 BC. The instrument became very popular early in the twentieth century when steel reeds began to be used, and a true piano keyboard added.

Concertina
English physicist Sir Charles Wheatstone invented the concertina in 1829. Bellows are compressed between two hand-held hexagonal button keyboards. These control the passage of air to free reeds which make the notes. Often used by folk dancers, it has a strident sound which carries in the open air.

Harmonica or mouth organ
The modern harmonica has a metal casing containing free reeds in channels leading to the side of the instrument. It is played by blowing or sucking, and a finger-operated slider switches to a second set of reeds. Used in folk or rock music, Vaughan Williams and Malcolm Arnold have also written concertos for the harmonica.

Bagpipes

In a bagpipe the sound is made by a double reed, and the notes controlled by finger-holes. But the player doesn't blow directly into the pipe, breathing instead into a bag (although this is sometimes filled by bellows) which is then squeezed under the arm, forcing the required amount of air into the pipe, known as the *chanter*. Modern bagpipes also have extra tubes called *drones* which provide a continuous harmony.

The bagpipe is an ancient instrument which may have existed by the first century AD. It is also geographically widespread. Although we tend to think of it as being Scottish, it is still in use all over Europe and also in many other parts of the world.

Profile

Size: 72 cm to 235 cm

Made of: sheep or goatskin (bag); bamboo, horn, wood, ivory, plastic (pipes)

Sound made by: double reed (chanter), single reed (drone)

First example: prehistoric

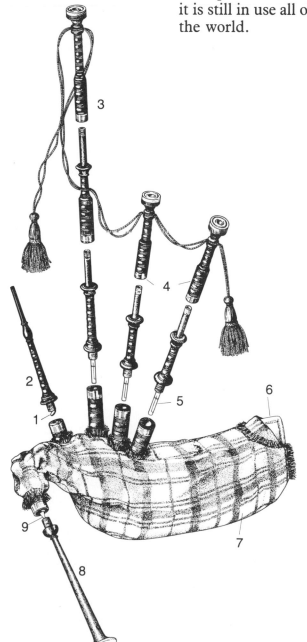

14th-century bagpipe player

Left: Exploded diagram of a Scottish highland bagpipe. **1** non-return valve; **2** blowpipe; **3** bass drone; **4** tenor drones; **5** drone reeds; **6** bag; **7** cover; **8** chanter; **9** chanter reed

Woodwind terms

air column: length of air contained in pipe which vibrates to make the sound. It may be shortened by opening *side holes*.

alto: range of notes sung by lowest female voice (as in alto saxophone)

baritone: range of notes sung by medium-range male voice (as in baritone saxophone)

barrel: section of instrument between mouthpiece and head joint, often adjustable for tuning purposes

bass: range of notes sung by lowest male voice (as in bass clarinet)

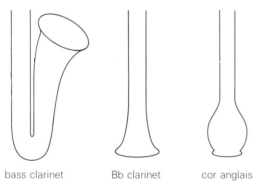

bass clarinet   Bb clarinet   cor anglais

bell: end of instrument furthest from the player. It usually widens out, but in some instruments is pear-shaped or globular.

bellows: expansible device, often made of leather, sometimes used to provide wind for instruments in place of the player's breath

block: the fipple, or stop in a whistle mouthpiece, preventing air from entering the instrument other than by the narrow passage which will ensure it hits the *lip*

bore: diameter of pipe

butt: lowest part of a bassoon containing a tube joining together the long joint and the wing joint and sometimes other useful devices like those enabling the instrument to be tuned or drained of excess moisture

chanter: pipe carrying the finger-holes in a bagpipe

crook: bent metal tube leading into the top of an instrument's main tube

double reed: a reed bent over on itself, secured to a *staple* and cut at the top to form two reeds which can then vibrate together when blown through

drone: pipe and reed (usually single) sounding only a single note in a bagpipe

duct flute: a *fipple* flute

edge-tone: sound resulting from an air stream being split on hitting a sharp edge or *lip*

embouchure: 1 player's lips and associated muscles, or mouth technique; 2 mouth-hole of transverse flute

finger-hole: side-hole controlled by the tip of the finger

fipple: block in the end of a whistle mouthpiece

flue-blown flute: flute blown from the end, not from the side

foot joint: section of tubing farthest away from the player, before the bell

free reed: reed, usually of metal, fastened only at one end

head joint: section of tubing closest to player, which also contains the embouchure in the transverse flute

key: sprung lever covering side-hole at one end, operated by finger at the other

key system: system of keys producing notes with greatest effect and ease *keywork:* the layout of keys on an instrument

ligature: device with one or two screws securing single reed to mouthpiece

lip: sharp edge of an *edge-tone* instrument's mouthpiece or mouth-hole

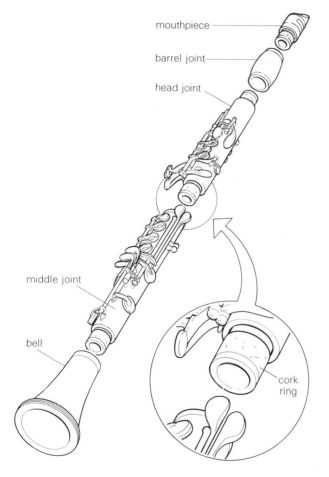

mouthpiece

barrel joint

head joint

middle joint

bell

cork ring

middle joint: the length of tubing between the *head joint* and the *foot joint*

mouth-hole: hole in the side of a transverse flute blown across by player

mouthpiece: section of an instrument carrying either the single reed or fipple etc, blown by player

octave key: key which assists the production of an octave when *overblowing*

overblowing: increasing the speed of the breath so as to play higher notes

pipe: tube of a wind instrument

plug: stopper at upper end of pipe to stop the air escaping in the wrong direction

profile: cross-section along the tube of a wind (or brass) instrument

resonator: empty chamber amplifying the sound made, for example by a free reed

side-hole: hole in the side of a tube

soprano: range of notes sung by highest female voice (as in soprano saxophone)

staple: thin metal tube to which a double reed is attached

sub-leader: the violinist sitting next to the leader of the orchestra

tenor: range of notes sung by highest adult male voice

tonguing: giving a clean start to detached notes or the first notes of phrases by 1 drawing the tongue sharply back from the reed whilst blowing (reed instruments), or 2 making a 't' sound behind the upper teeth (flutes)

transposing instrument: one in which notes sound at pitches other than those at which they are written

transverse flute: flute played crosswise (as opposed to a *duct flute*)

treble: range of notes sung by highest boy's voice (as in treble recorder)

whistle mouthpiece: mouthpiece of type used in fipple flutes, recorders etc and other types of duct flute

Here are some of the woodwind instruments playing together in groups in which they are often heard

Highland pipers from Scotland

Ganda notched-flute players in an ensemble from Uganda

A woodwind ensemble or wind band, which also includes two french horns

Brass

Some instruments in use today

Most brass instruments really are made of *brass*, an alloy of copper and zinc. They occasionally look as though other materials have been used, although usually the brass has been *lacquered* or silver-plated to make maintenance easier.

Many brass instruments are *transposing instruments*. They are described as, for example, 'in B flat' or 'in F'. This tells us the lowest note which they play on their *open tubing* – when none of their valves are being used. Brass players often have to play instruments in different keys but to make things easier they learn only one set of fingering, as if all their instruments were in the same key: C. This means that the music from which they play has to be adjusted, or *transposed*, according to which instrument they're playing. Usually this is done when the music is written or printed, but sometimes the players have to transpose as they are playing.

1 piccolo trumpet
2 Bb trumpet
3 bass trumpet
4 Bb cornet
5 Bb flugel horn
6 tenor trombone
7 Bb/F/E bass trombone
8 F/Bb double horn
9 Eb horn
10 Bb baritone
11 Bb euphonium
12 CC tuba
13 bass Wagner tuba
14 BBb sousaphone

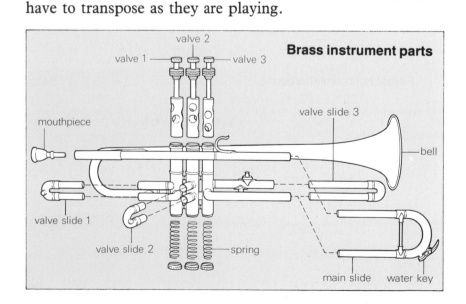

Brass instrument parts

valve 1 — valve 2 — valve 3

mouthpiece

valve slide 3

bell

valve slide 1

valve slide 2

spring

main slide

water key

What makes the sound?

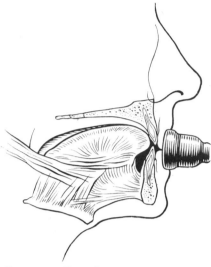

Cross-section of a trumpet player's mouth, showing tongue and lip positions

Brass instrument mouthpieces

Horn mouthpiece

Flugel horn mouthpiece

As in woodwind instruments, the sound is made by the vibration of the air column within the instrument. But the player's own lips form the reed. They themselves vibrate and start the movement of the air column. The combination of lips and mouthpiece is known as a *lip-reed*.

How does the player make different notes?
Air in a tube vibrates not only as a whole but also in fractions of its length at the same time. Since a shorter vibrating air column gives a higher note, the fractions give higher notes than the whole.

The note produced by the vibrations of the entire column is called the *fundamental*. The notes given by the vibrating fractions are *harmonics*. Only one series of harmonics can be obtained from an air column of given length: the *harmonic series*. All brass instruments work on this principle.

The player's lips rest on a cup-shaped mouthpiece, and breathing out sets them vibrating. The exact moment the vibrations begin is controlled by the tongue being quickly withdrawn from behind the upper teeth. By adjusting the tension of the lips, the player can make them vibrate at the frequency (that is, the speed) of the harmonic that is to be played.

Slacker lips vibrate more slowly, tighter lips more quickly. lower notes are also more easily played if the speed of the breath is reduced, and higher notes if the speed is increased.

Tuba mouthpiece

Harmonic series on a Bb fundamental

Harmonic no:

6 Vibrating thirty-seconds at 3680 cps

5 Vibrating sixteenths at 1840 cps

4 Vibrating eighths at 920 cps

3 Vibrating quarters at 460 cps

2 Vibrating halves at 230 cps

1 (Fundamental) entire length vibrating at (approx) 115 cps

Brass instrument profiles

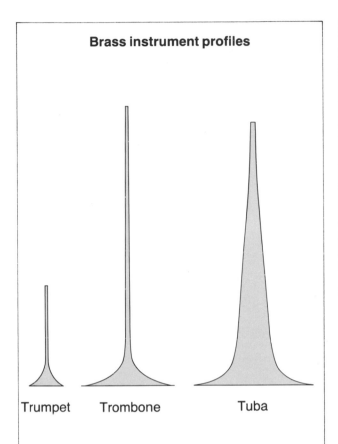

Trumpet Trombone Tuba

The more cylindrical *profiles* of the trumpet and trombone give a brilliant tone. As the tubes become more conical the sound becomes broader and smoother. This is assisted by proportionately larger *bells*.

Brass instrument shapes

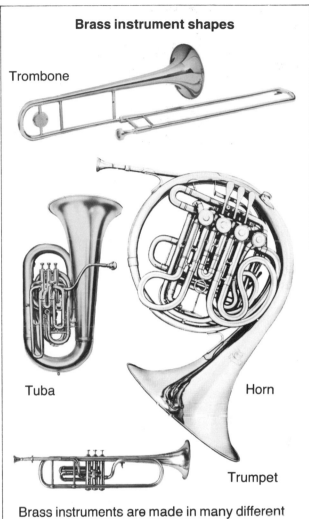

Trombone

Tuba Horn

Trumpet

Brass instruments are made in many different shapes. Here are examples of them, not to scale.

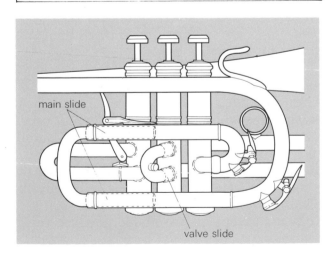

main slide

valve slide

Tuning slides

So that the instruments may be *tuned* to the other members of the band or orchestra, a device is needed to tune the whole instrument. This needs to be easily adjustable, but to stay put when adjusted, so each has a U-shaped *main slide* which makes the overall length of tubing shorter (giving slightly higher notes) or longer (giving slightly lower notes). The loop of tubing controlled by each *valve* also has a small adjustable slide, a *valve slide*, so that it may be individually tuned.

The slide

Since different lengths of air column produce different harmonic series, a tube which can be made longer or shorter at will can produce many more notes than one which is of fixed length.

The trombone uses a *slide* to achieve this.

Seven different harmonic series can be obtained in steps of half a tone, and when they are written down as music, they appear as in the diagram. By moving the slide from one *position* to another, all the notes shown on the diagram can be produced in any order.

Harmonic series of tenor trombone

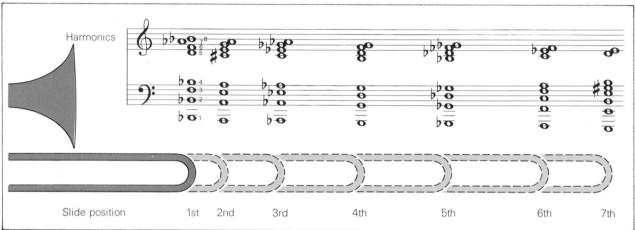

The fundamental of each harmonic series (no. 1) is playable on most of the deeper instruments. It is known as a *pedal note*. The actual number of harmonics which can be obtained depends entirely on how good the player is. Professional brass players can usually obtain at least eleven or twelve, and often many more. Harmonic 8 is usually too out of tune to be used, but in his *Serenade for Tenor, Horn and Strings* Benjamin Britten exploited this for special effect.

The valve

As an alternative to the slide, it would be possible to make more notes available by providing a player with a number of tubes of different lengths which could be used as required. This was the principle of the omnitonic horn. The 'plumber's nightmare' was in reality eight horns wound side by side, the player choosing the tube of appropriate length to put the mouthpiece into and play.

All brass instruments except the trombone now use valves to provide extra harmonic series.

Omnitonic horn of 1815

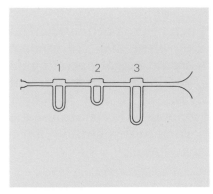

Tubing with 3 valves

The standard number of valves is three. They may be used singly or in combination.

Each valve controls an extra length of tubing. The length of air column added by valve no. 2 lowers the harmonic series of the open instrument (that is, the tube without added valves) by half a tone; no. 1 lowers it by a tone; no. 3 lowers it 1½ tones. The various combinations produce the same effect as the positions of the trombone slide. Compare the euphonium's harmonic series below with those of the trombone opposite.

Harmonic series of the euphonium

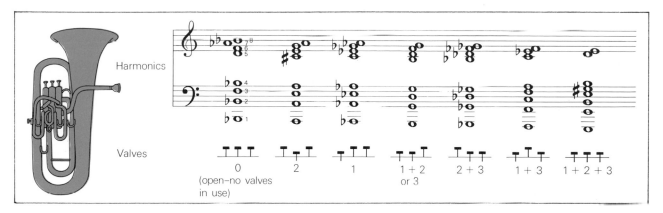

Some brass instruments have more than three valves. When there is a fourth valve it normally lowers the instrument's open harmonic series to fill the gap between the lowest second harmonic and the highest pedal note. Some larger tubas have up to six valves, all helping to give deeper notes.

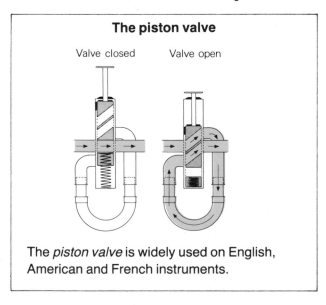

The piston valve

Valve closed   Valve open

The *piston valve* is widely used on English, American and French instruments.

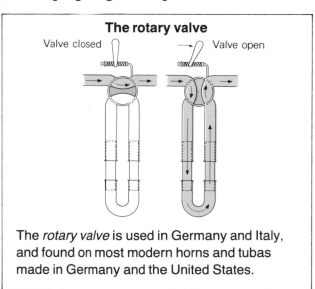

The rotary valve

Valve closed   Valve open

The *rotary valve* is used in Germany and Italy, and found on most modern horns and tubas made in Germany and the United States.

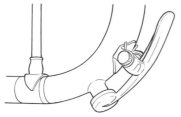

The water key drains the instrument of water created by condensation of breath.

Compensation

Each of valves 1 to 3 lowers the pitch of the open instrument by ½/1/1½ tones respectively. But when they are used in conjunction with each other they are no longer operating on the length of the *open* instrument, but on the open instrument plus one or two of the other valves, and so they no longer lower the pitch by quite the same amount. This is because the added tubing is too short in proportion to that already in use to produce a note exactly half a tone lower.

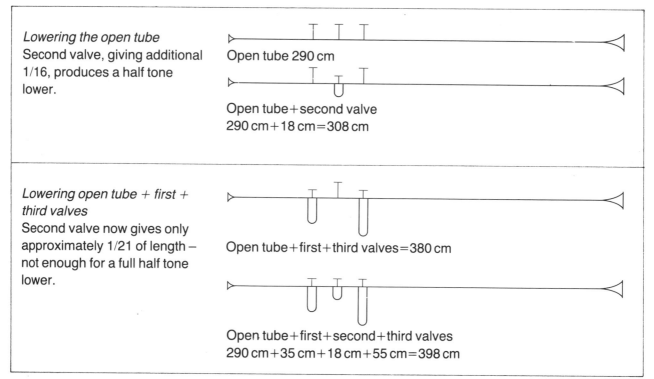

Lowering the open tube
Second valve, giving additional 1/16, produces a half tone lower.

Open tube 290 cm

Open tube + second valve
290 cm + 18 cm = 308 cm

Lowering open tube + first + third valves
Second valve now gives only approximately 1/21 of length – not enough for a full half tone lower.

Open tube + first + third valves = 380 cm

Open tube + first + second + third valves
290 cm + 35 cm + 18 cm + 55 cm = 398 cm

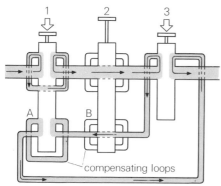

The system of compensating loops, showing how when valves 1 and 3 are pressed the loops on valve 1 work. The loops on valve 2 work if 1, 2 and 3 are pressed.

Trumpets, with a relatively short length of open tubing, often have a third valve slide which can be easily slid out by the player during performance, increasing the air column length. Alternatively there may be levers on the first and third valve slides. These *triggers* enable them to be instantly extended to add the necessary length to keep the instrument in tune when more than one valve is being used.

Larger instruments, from the euphonium down, are often *compensated* on a system invented by David Blaikley in 1874. This sends the air stream round an extra set of valve slides when the third valve (in three-valve instruments) or fourth valve (in four-valve instruments) is operated, adding the necessary extra length of air column to keep the notes in tune.

Compensated horns, which are not the same, are described in the section on the horn.

Some very early brass players

The tuba, or straight Roman trumpet used by the infantry, was about 125 cm long.

Left: The celtic carnyx had an ox horn for a bell. It dates from the Second Iron Age.

Trumpet players during the Pythian Games in Ancient Greece 'were overjoyed when they found they had neither rent their cheeks, nor burst their blood vessels, by their exertions, and they used a *capistrum*, or bandage . . . for the purpose of preventing their cheeks from swelling'. Stafford, *History of Music*, 1830.

The lur was usually made from bronze and was the most important instrument in Northern Europe during the Bronze Age.

The curved cornu was played in Roman processions. Made of a bronze tube bent round into a G-shape, it had a wooden bar fitted across to act as a grip.

Cup mouthpieces, finger-holes and keys

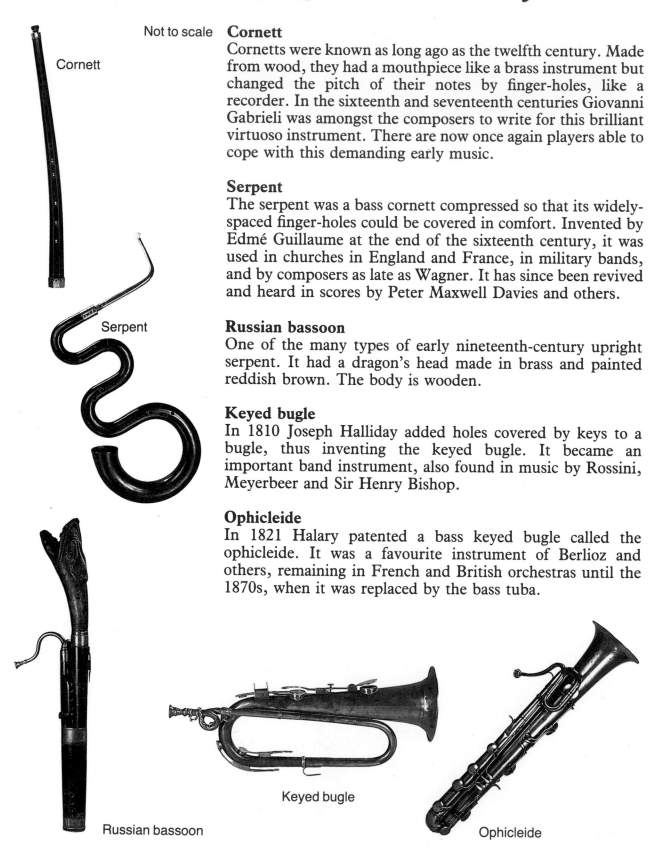

Not to scale

Cornett

Serpent

Russian bassoon

Keyed bugle

Ophicleide

Cornett

Cornetts were known as long ago as the twelfth century. Made from wood, they had a mouthpiece like a brass instrument but changed the pitch of their notes by finger-holes, like a recorder. In the sixteenth and seventeenth centuries Giovanni Gabrieli was amongst the composers to write for this brilliant virtuoso instrument. There are now once again players able to cope with this demanding early music.

Serpent

The serpent was a bass cornett compressed so that its widely-spaced finger-holes could be covered in comfort. Invented by Edmé Guillaume at the end of the sixteenth century, it was used in churches in England and France, in military bands, and by composers as late as Wagner. It has since been revived and heard in scores by Peter Maxwell Davies and others.

Russian bassoon

One of the many types of early nineteenth-century upright serpent. It had a dragon's head made in brass and painted reddish brown. The body is wooden.

Keyed bugle

In 1810 Joseph Halliday added holes covered by keys to a bugle, thus inventing the keyed bugle. It became an important band instrument, also found in music by Rossini, Meyerbeer and Sir Henry Bishop.

Ophicleide

In 1821 Halary patented a bass keyed bugle called the ophicleide. It was a favourite instrument of Berlioz and others, remaining in French and British orchestras until the 1870s, when it was replaced by the bass tuba.

Instruments with single harmonic series

Post horn
This is the type of instrument shown in many European Post Office documents.

British regimental bugle
The tubing of the compact regimental bugle is wound round twice with a small bell.

Alphorn
With a cup mouthpiece, but made from wood, the longest known alphorn was heard in West Germany and was 10 m in length. These examples are Swiss.

Oliphant
Made from an elephant's tusk, this precious oliphant was decorated by its proud owner.

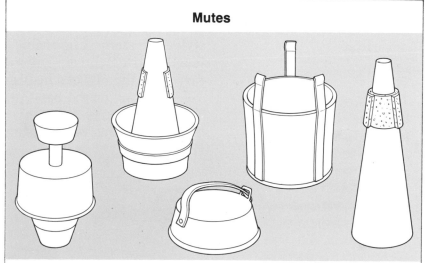

Mutes

Mutes, made from metal, plastic, fibre or compressed cardboard, fit into, or in some cases over, the bell of a brass instrument. They change the tone. Almost all modern brass instruments use straight mutes, but many more types are available for trumpet and trombone including *cup, plunger,* and *harmon* mutes.

Trombone

Profile
Size: alto, 86 cm long; tenor,
114 cm long; bass, 115 cm
long
Made of: brass
Sound made by *lip-reed*
First example: probably
Italy, 15th century

An angel with a trombone
(accompanied by a dulcimer)
painted in the late 15th century by
Filippino Lippi

The old English name for
trombone was 'sackbut',
from the Spanish
sacabuche, a boat's hand-
pump. 'Trombone' comes
from the Italian *tromba*
('trumpet') and -*one*,
meaning 'a large version'.

'Mr Mariotti the celebrated
trombone player is now in
his 85th year and has not left
off puffing yet.'
The Musical World, 28 July
1837.

During the middle ages, as longer trumpets were made, to produce lower notes, it became customary to bend the tube into an S-shape. The instruments were then more convenient to handle. It was only a step to arrange for one section to slide inside the other so that the total length of the tubing could be changed, giving additional harmonic series.

By the sixteenth century the trombone was well known, playing beside cornetts, viols and particularly voices, which it accompanied sympathetically. Only minor changes have been made in design during the past 400 years.

There was a complete family of trombones: *treble*, *alto*, *tenor*, *bass* and *contrabass*. The treble was replaced by the trumpet, which can play the same notes (and more) much more satisfactorily. The alto is still used for the high trombone parts written by Schumann, Beethoven and Gluck.

The most common trombone is the tenor, which often has a rotary valve known as the *plug* or *trigger* bringing into operation extra tubing to fill the gap (except for one note) between the highest pedal note and lowest second harmonic. This tenor-bass trombone is sometimes called the B flat/F trombone as the first position of the slide gives F with the valve in operation.

The modern bass trombone is a wider-bore version of this instrument, often with a second valve enabling the missing note to be played. It also covers the lowest range heard in many Wagner operas.

Symphony orchestras and bands normally include three trombones: two tenors and a bass. They can play in many styles. It seems impossible that the solemn chords in the fourth movement of Brahms's Fourth Symphony could be played by the raucous instruments heard in Rossini's *William Tell Overture*, or the band prankster of pieces like *The Joker*. This solo features the trombone's ability to play a *glissando* – a slide from one note to another, taking in all the notes between.

The oldest surviving trombone,
made in Germany in 1551 by
Erasmus Schnitzer

Although it is often stated that the first symphony to include trombones was Beethoven's Fifth (1807), Franz Beck included three in his Symphony in Eb, composed about 1760.

Trombones can be very exciting, as in Wagner's 'Ride of the Valkyrie'. They can also be very serious, even noble. Mendelssohn thought they should be kept for special occasions, like the moment in Mozart's *Don Giovanni* when a statue comes to life. They have been used since their earliest days in sacred music. There is a trombone solo in the 'Tuba Mirum' of Mozart's *Requiem*, and a trombone intones a chant in Rimsky-Korsakov's *Russian Easter Festival* Overture. The difficult high solo in Ravel's *Bolero* was influenced by the smooth style of dance band playing.

Trombones are frequently heard in jazz. In New Orleans the rough sounds of the 'tailgate trombone' (so called because it had to face over the tailgate when the band was playing on a cart) were very familiar. During the 1960s many jazz trombonists turned to valve trombones so as to play the fast notes in bebop (a style of modern jazz), although the phenomenal 'J J' Johnson coped admirably with a slide trombone.

Valve trombones are popular in military bands in some European countries, especially Italy where composers like Verdi used them in the orchestra during the nineteenth century.

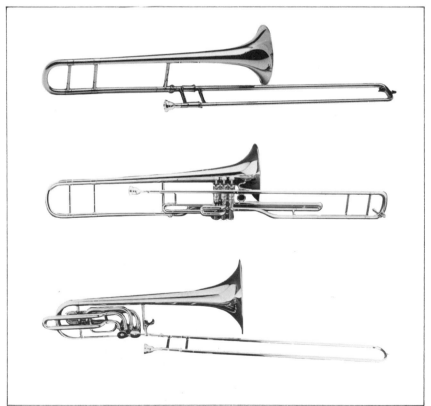

Top: Tenor trombone. Middle: Valve trombone. Bottom: Bass trombone.

Trumpet

Profile
Size: piccolo trumpet, 37 cm;
D trumpet, 46 cm; Bb
trumpet, 48 cm
Made of: brass
Sound made by: lip-reed
First example: natural,
Egypt, 2000 BC; valved,
Germany, about 1827

A natural trumpet of 1667 by
Beale, which is an early example
of an English trumpet

Trumpets and trombones have mainly cylindrical tubing, like the prehistoric canes and hollow branches in which they originated.

The brilliant sound of the trumpet has always been associated with pomp, ceremony and royalty. So exclusive was the instrument felt to be that in the middle ages guilds of trumpeters were formed, jealously protecting their art and excluding those thought not suitable for membership.

In the time of Monteverdi, Bach and Handel, when trumpets had no valves and could therefore sound only one harmonic series, specialists played the difficult *clarino* parts using the trumpet's highest harmonics, which lie so close to each other that melodies are possible. Their art had died out by the late eighteenth century, and trumpet parts of the Mozart and Beethoven period consist mainly of long *bugle-call* notes. The first valve trumpet was made in 1826, but composers continued to write parts for the *natural* (valveless) trumpet for several decades after that.

For many years the standard trumpet in many countries has been pitched in B flat, like the B flat clarinet. In France the trumpet in C, one tone higher, has been favoured. The D trumpet, one tone higher still, is often used for playing high parts: much of Bach and Handel (including *The Trumpet Shall Sound*) and more recent music like Ravel's *Bolero* and Britten's *Peter Grimes*.

A smaller trumpet still, known as the piccolo trumpet, pitched in B flat an octave above the normal, is used for the extremely high and difficult parts in music like Bach's *Brandenburg Concerto no. 2* and the Beatles' *Penny Lane*.

In an attempt to complete the family of trumpets, Wagner introduced the bass trumpet into the orchestra for his opera series *The Ring of the Nibelung*. It is pitched in C or B flat, like the tenor trombone.

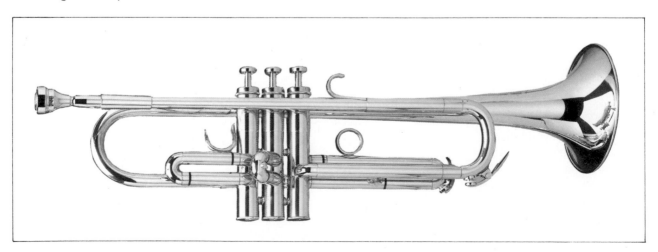

In the Polish city of Krakow, a trumpeter from the fire brigade band is stationed in a high tower of St Mary's Church to sound a call every hour. It finishes in the middle of a note, where the town trumpeter was halted by an arrow from the invading Tartar army in the 10th century.

The trumpet is important in jazz. It often plays the melody in New Orleans and Chicago jazz, and in the hands of musicians like Miles Davis and Dizzy Gillespie has been made to achieve amazing and beautiful effects. Trumpets are also found in sections of three or four in 'big bands' and dance bands, while symphonic wind bands often contain both trumpets and cornets.

The most famous trumpet concertos are those by Haydn (composed in 1796 for an unsuccessful keyed trumpet) and Hummel.

The brilliance of the trumpet's tone enables it to lead either the brass section or the entire orchestra with ease. Two, three, and sometimes four are found in a symphony orchestra. They are prominent in works like Ravel's *Daphnis and Chloe* and Dvořák's 'New World' Symphony. Verdi used four trumpets in the orchestra for his *Requiem* which at the 'Tuba Mirum' ('Last Trump') play a thrilling fanfare with four more placed in another part of the concert hall. The twelve trumpets in Janáček's *Sinfonietta* provide more exciting moments. But there is also a mysterious side to the instrument, as you can hear in 'Fêtes', from Debussy's *Nocturnes*, where three quiet muted trumpets provide one of music's most magical moments.

Jazz trumpeter Dizzy Gillespie playing his 'bent horn', a trumpet with a unique upturned bell

A fanfare being sounded by the famous Kneller Hall Trumpeters from the Royal Military School of Music

The *shofar*, a ram's horn used in the synagogue

This type of slide trumpet, used in England in the 19th century, had a slide which pulled towards the player, lowering the harmonic series by a tone.

Horn

Horns have more conical tubing than trumpets and trombones, giving a broad, smooth sound. This is assisted by the mouthpiece which is more conical than cup-shaped.

Originally used in hunting, they were first heard in an English orchestra in about 1717, in Handel's *Water Music*, playing the notes of their single harmonic series. Around the same time *crooks* were invented. These are circles of tubing of different lengths which enable alternative harmonic series to be played when joined to the instrument's own tube.

In the middle of the eighteenth century, Anton Hampel of Dresden obtained different notes by putting his hand into the bell of the horn and changing its position. He thus made it possible to play scales and tunes, although they were more satisfactorily performed after the invention of the valve (about 1814) by the horn player Heinrich Stölzel.

Players support the horn by the right hand in the bell.

'I would remark that I have heard a fantasia played by Mr Perry . . . upon a *horn with valves or plugs* . . . I should think this a very valuable idea.'
Letter from 'Semiquaver' in *The Musical World*, 17 March 1837.

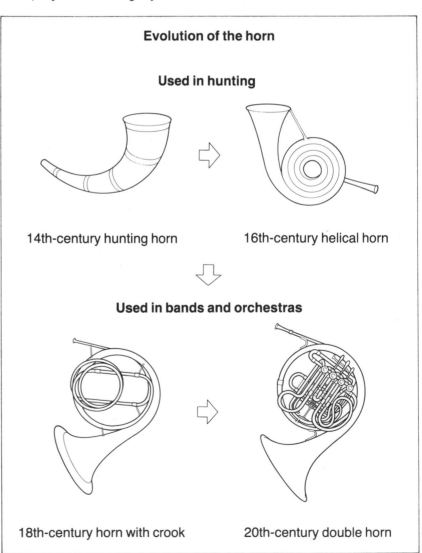

Evolution of the horn

Used in hunting

14th-century hunting horn

16th-century helical horn

Used in bands and orchestras

18th-century horn with crook

20th-century double horn

Russian horn band

There were up to 100 members in these 18th and early 19th-century bands, each playing only one or two notes. Melodies were performed by combining the notes of hunting horns varying in length from 30 cm to 200 cm.

The french horn (thought to have originated in France) is normally in F, but to help avoid using the higher harmonics, nowadays almost all players use horns made in Germany pitched in F and B flat. Full double horns are in effect two instruments in one with separate valve slides for the F and B flat 'sides', while in compensated double horns, tubing is added to the B flat valve slides for the F side. There are various other combinations of double and even triple horns, designed to cater for players' special requirements. Some have as many as five valves.

By playing one note and humming another it is possible to make a brass instrument sound two or three notes at the same time. The 19th-century horn player Eugène Vivier was fond of this trick, until an innkeeper charged him for the three guests heard practising in his room!

Mozart wrote four famous concertos for horn, and Richard Strauss wrote two more. The romantic and evocative sound of the horn can be heard in much nineteenth and twentieth century music.

There are solos in Weber's *Der Freischütz* Overture, Tchaikovsky's Fifth Symphony, the 'Nocturne' from Mendelssohn's music to *A Midsummer Night's Dream*, and horn calls galore in Wagner's *The Ring of the Nibelung*. With the hand tightly stopping the instrument, and blown hard, the *cuivré* effect is produced, heard in much of Debussy's orchestral music. The horn can also whoop with joy – an effect often used by Malcolm Arnold and Richard Strauss.

There are normally four horns in the modern orchestra, plus a 'bumper' lending support to the first horn player. More horns are quite often needed (ten in Schoenberg's *Gurrelieder*).

Horns are found in most wind bands, one is included in both wind and brass quintets, and they are often heard in more sumptuous 'big bands'. The horn was first used in jazz in the Claude Thornhill Band of the 1940s.

The Background Brass

Profile: Flugel horn
Size: 40 cm long.
Made of: brass.
Sound made by: lip-reed.
First example: Austria, about
1820

Jazz player Freddie Hubbard
demonstrating the flugel horn

Profile: Eb horn
Size: 45 cm high.
Made of: brass.
Sound made by: lip-reed.
First example: Austria, about
1820

This is a large group of instruments found more often in bands than in orchestras. With the exception of the euphonium, they play mainly music which provides a rhythm or harmony supporting the melody. This is why they are sometimes called the background brass. They were perfected and made into a matching family by the inventor of the saxophone, Adolphe Sax, between 1843 and 1855. He named the instruments the saxhorns, a name still sometimes used, especially in France.

These instruments have even more widely conical tubes than the horn, with consequently very broad, smooth tones. Their ancestor was the horn of the young bullock, the bugle. Since they all now have valves, the family is also called the valved bugle horns.

As the names used for different sizes in various countries are sometimes confusing, these are given in each case.

Flugel horn

(UK: flugel horn; USA: fluegel horn; Germany: flügelhorn in B; France: bugle si flat)

The flugel horn's ancestor was a German bugle used for signalling by each wing, or *Flügel*, of beaters during hunting. It is in the shape of a trumpet with three valves, and in Britain and the USA pitched in B flat, like the normal trumpet. In European bands, however, many other pitches are used.

The tone of the instrument is mellower and less incisive than the trumpet or cornet, and composers have made use of this softer sound in writing solo passages for flugel horn.

There is an important solo in Vaughan Williams' Ninth Symphony, and flugel horns are used in works by Respighi also. One is found in each British brass band, and it is often heard in modern jazz. Jazz trumpeters often double on the flugel horn following its popularising by Miles Davis in the 1950s.

E flat horn

(UK: tenor horn; USA: alto horn; Germany: althorn; France: alto)

The E flat is the smallest saxhorn made in tuba shape. It has three valves, and its range means it can play five notes lower than the flugel horn and four notes higher than the baritone. Unlike the larger members of the family, the E flat horn is small and light enough to be carried easily by its player. For marching bands, most of the bigger background brass are supported by a sling round the player's neck. There are three E flat horns in British brass bands, but they are never used in the orchestra, and French horns are preferred in wind bands.

Profile: Baritone
Size: 67 cm high.
Made of: brass.
Sound made by: lip-reed.
First example: Austria, about
1820

Baritone

(UK: baritone; USA: baritone horn; Germany: tenorhorn; France: baryton).

Mahler's Seventh Symphony begins with an important solo for baritone – the only time it appears in the orchestra, except in an offstage band in Respighi's *Pines of Rome*. The baritone is important in bands, however, especially in the United States, where there is so much confusion between baritone and euphonium that some makers market instruments of the same size under two different names. Baritones are like large E flat horns, playing notes four below. Listen out for baritone with tuba in American television cartoon music.

Euphonium

(UK: euphonium; USA: euphonium; Germany: baryton; France: basse).

Called 'the cello of the band', the euphonium is the most important of the deeper instruments in bands of all sorts. It was invented by Herr Sommer of Weimar about 1843 and made a great impression when played by him at the 1851 Great Exhibition in London with organ accompaniment. The euphonium has three, or more often four, valves (making more notes available). Like the baritone, it is in B flat, an octave below the trumpet, but it has a much wider bore, which gives a full and impressive tone. It is equally at home playing bass or tenor parts. It sometimes appears in the orchestra, usually under the name tenor tuba. Holst's suite *The Planets*, Richard Strauss's *Don Quixote* and *Ein Heldenleben*, Janáček's *Sinfonietta* and works by Shostakovich, Respighi, Meyerbeer and Verdi need euphonium. Quite often it is used to play parts originally written for ophicleide.

Profile: Euphonium
Size 68 cm high.
Made of: brass.
Sound made by: lip-reed.
First example: Germany,
about 1843

Tuba

Profile
Size: 65-122 cm high
Made of: brass
Sound made by: lip-reed
First example: Germany, 1835

Bandmaster Wilhelm Wieprecht invented the bass tuba in 1835 because, as he wrote: 'For ten years now I have been working with military bands, and I have felt, I suppose, most sorely the need of a true contrabass wind instrument'.

Tubas are found in all sorts of bands, usually under the name of bass, or (printed on the music), bombardon. They are found in symphony orchestras, rarely more than one at a time, though Berlioz required as many as four. Modern tubas have from three to six valves. In British orchestras the EE flat is standard, in the United States it is the CC. Players often use the F and BB flat tubas where composers require a particular effect.

The many types of tuba

Bass tubas
F tuba: tuba pitched in F, four notes below the euphonium. E♭ tuba: medium narrow-bore tuba in E♭ with three valves. EE♭ tuba (an octave lower): wider-bore tuba with four valves.

Contrabass tubas
CC tuba: tuba in C, four notes below F tuba. BB♭ tuba pitched an octave below euphonium.

Below left: Part of an orchestral brass section with the tuba in the foreground

Below right: A tuba being played in an orchestra with a mute in the bell

Bass tuba by J G Moritz, dating from about 1838, three years after the instrument was invented

The tuba has solos from time to time: in Mahler's First Symphony, Stravinsky's *Petrouchka*, Malcolm Arnold's Harmonica Concerto, Shostakovich's Thirteenth Symphony and Gershwin's *American in Paris*, for example. The solo in Ravel's orchestration of Mussorgsky's *Pictures from an Exhibition* is normally played on the euphonium.

There are several concertos for tuba, most importantly one by Vaughan Williams, and a unique piece with narrator, Kleinsinger's *Tubby the Tuba*.

The tuba's contribution to jazz is not restricted now to its role in early bands, where it was often substituted for the double bass. On early jazz records this substitution was needed, as the recording equipment found it hard to pick up the sound of the string instrument. From this 'oompah' role, with such players as Pete Briggs (with Louis Armstrong's Hot Seven), jazz composers and arrangers developed the use of the tuba. Stan Kenton wrote for the tuba in his orchestrations, and Howard Johnson, of the American Gil Evans band is a virtuoso player.

Some large tubas

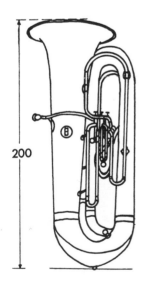

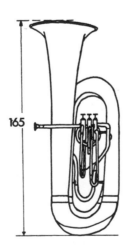

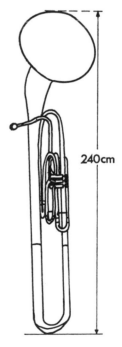

Subcontrabass tuba made in 1896-98 by the firm of Boosey

Sax-bourdon mib made by Adolphe Sax in 1851

A tuba used in the 1928 production of a musical. It was played by a musician standing in the orchestra pit

Cornet

Profile
Size: 35 cm long
Made of: brass
Sound made by: lip-reed
First example: France, late 1820s
Relations: post horn

Above: A cornetist
Below: The same player just behind a trumpeter, showing the contrasting shapes of the two instruments

Rude remarks on the cornet:
'Coarse and vulgar'
Prout, 1897
'The instrument which needs least study and is most vulgar'
Lavignac, 1895

Like many of the other brass, the cornet came into existence when valves were added to an earlier type of instrument – in this case, the small circular post horn used on the Continent.

The cornet's tubing is between the trumpet's and flugel horn's in profile, making it easier to play but giving it a tone which has more often been criticised than praised. Malcolm Arnold, in *Beckus the Dandiprat*, and Stravinsky in *Petrouchka* used the cornet as soloist simply because of its lowly associations.

It is pitched in B flat, like the trumpet, and has always been the leading brass melody and solo instrument in bands. In France cornets had valves before trumpets, so many composers wrote for cornet rather than trumpet. At the same time, trumpet parts were often played on the cornet, not sounding quite so grand, and all helped to give the cornet a bad name.

Some composers, like Berlioz and Tchaikovsky, used cornets alongside trumpets in the orchestra (the cornet solo in the 'Waltz' from *Swan Lake* is well known), but they remain mainly band instruments. Many of the early jazz players, like Buddy Bolden, Bunk Johnson and King Oliver, played cornet, although it takes no real part in modern jazz.

The only known photograph showing the legendary Buddy 'King' Bolden, an early New Orleans jazz cornetist, who is standing on the left of the picture

Some unusual brass instruments

Wagner tuba

A cross between horn and tuba, the Wagner tuba is always used in sets of four, two tenors and two basses. They are played by horn players, using conical horn-type mouthpieces, and were the idea of Wagner, who wrote for them in *The Ring of the Nibelung*. Stravinsky and Bruckner are amongst several other composers who have used them. They were also heard in the MoTown Sound of the 1960s and some film and television scores.

Helicon and sousaphone

The helicon is a bass tuba made in a round shape, probably first of all in Russia about 1845. The bell rests on the player's left shoulder. In 1898 the American bandmaster John Philip Sousa designed the sousaphone which is in a similar shape. The massive bell is nowadays made from fibreglass to reduce the weight.

A bass Wagner tuba. The mouthpiece is hidden by the bell.

A tenor cor or mellophone made in 1931

Duplex instruments

A duplex instrument is really two in one, the player is able to choose which one to blow into by means of a valve. The first was made in 1851, and the most popular was a combined euphonium and valve trombone.

Tenor cor and mellophone

The tenor cor (American: mellophone) is in the shape of a french horn, but as it has half the tube length is pitched an octave higher. It therefore uses lower harmonics to play in the same register as the french horn. This makes it less easy for the player to play the wrong note. It is used in brass bands and can be made to sound quite like the french horn.

A modern B♭ sousaphone. At first the bell pointed upwards, but it now faces forwards over the player's head. There are three and four-valve versions.

Brass terms

alto: range of notes sung by lowest female voice (played by alto trombone etc)

ascending valve: valve cutting out tubing to raise pitch

background brass: the wide-bored, valved bugle horns

bass: range of notes sung by lowest male voice (played by bass trombone, etc)

bell: widening-out of tube at end farthest from player

bell-flare: abruptly widening extremity of bell

branch: any single length of tubing

brass: alloy of copper and zinc (about 70%/ 30% to 85%/15%)

bugle call: melody using notes nos. 2-6 of single harmonic series

clarino: high trumpet part, mainly of eighteenth century

compensated horn: horn with two tubes giving different harmonic series but with common valve slides

compensating system: mechanical method of avoiding faulty tuning resulting from the use of several valves at the same time.

contrabass: range of notes an octave below bass

crook: circle of extra tubing, usually inserted between mouthpiece and main tubing

cup mouthpiece: brass instrument mouthpiece, particularly of type other than horn

descending valve: valve adding tubing to lower pitch

double: a) octave lower (as in BB flat tuba); b) in two pitches (as in double horn in F/B flat)

embouchure: player's lips and muscles controlling them

fanfare: brass instrument flourish, especially for trumpets

finger-hole: hole in tubing, opened and closed by the player's finger

flutter tonguing: effect produced by rolling tongue (as in a rolled 'r') whilst blowing instrument

fundamental: lowest note of harmonic series

funnel mouthpiece: conical mouthpiece of horn

glissando: slide from one note to another of different pitch

harmon mute: two metal parts used in trumpet bell. Inner part is tube which slides inside outer shell. Produces very quiet sound, used for 'talking trumpet' and 'wa-wa' effects

harmonic: part of a harmonic series

harmonic series: series of harmonics obtainable from tube of given length

key: lever with pad covering hole in tube at one end, operated by finger at the other

lacquer: clear coating applied to brass instruments

lip-reed: lips vibrating in mouthpiece, causing vibration of the air column

main slide: U-shaped metal device linking player's lips to instrument's tubing

mute: device fitting into or over the bell to change the instrument's tone *natural*: a tube played without assistance from slide, valve or finger-holes

open: a) tube without additional valve tubing or, in trombone, lower slide position in operation; b) played without mute

pedal note: fundamental

piccolo: Italian for 'small'

piston valve: valve based on principle of sliding piston

plug: rotary valve of B flat/F trombone

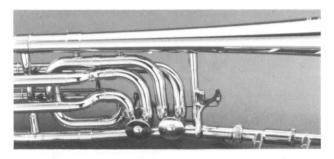

plunger mute or *cup mute*: named after plumber's sink plunger, this bowl shaped rubber or pasteboard mute is held over trumpet or trombone bell.

position: one of the seven extensions to trombone slide giving different harmonic series

profile: cross-section of 'unwound' tubing from end to end of instrument

rotary valve: valve based on principle of turning rotor

section: group of players of similar instruments (such as brass section, horn section)

slide: U-shaped tubing sliding outside or within two other lengths of tubing to change pitch

stay: metal strut, rod or pillar supporting branch or branches

straight mute: conical device of metal, plastic, or cardboard, inserted into bell of instrument, held in place by corks

tenor: range of notes of highest male voice (played by tenor trombone, etc)

tonguing: initiation of note by action of tongue

transposing instrument: one in which notes sound at pitches other than those at which they are written

transposed: music which has been adjusted to be played easily by a transposing instrument

treble: range of notes sung by the highest female, or boy's, voice (played by treble trombone etc)

tune: to tune an instrument is to make sure that it is playing at exactly the right pitch – neither sharp nor flat

tuning slide: slide enabling player to tune either the whole instrument or one valve at a time

valve: device controlling admission of air to additional tubing

valve slide: tuning slide for individual valve

valve system: pattern of changes in total length of tubing produced by valves of an instrument

vibrato: rapid repeated small variation in pitch of note induced by embouchure or by moving the hand in the bell

water key: sprung lever allowing accumulated moisture to be drained from instrument through a small hole

Here are some of the settings in which brass instruments can be heard today.

A Salvation Army band concert, with cornets (left), trombones (right) and tubas (rear) surrounding the 'background brass'.

A British army Guards regimental band, showing in the foreground the variety of brass instruments in use.

An African 'horn' band playing lip-reed instruments made from dried gourds lashed together.

Percussion *Some instruments in use today*

1 castanets
2 wood blocks
3 temple block
4 tambourine
5 triangle
6 clash cymbals
7 suspended cymbal
8 hi-hat
9 tam-tam
10 bass drum
11 tom-toms
12 side drum
13 timpani
14 xylophone
15 glockenspiel
16 bell-lyra
17 antique cymbals
18 vibraphone
19 tubular bells

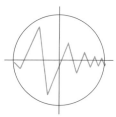

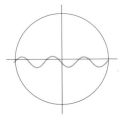

The percussion section is sometimes called 'the kitchen department.' Shakespeare refers to the percussive use of the tongs, bones and salt-box. Pots and pans were used at the time by the less well-off as makeshift instruments. The term passed to kettledrums with their bowls and cymbals reminiscent of pan lids.

If it makes a sound when you hit it, it could be a percussion instrument!

The first percussionists may have been prehistoric people who made rhythms by beating their chests or clapping their hands. A hollow tree trunk with the ends covered by animal skins may have been the first drum.

The modern percussion player, too, is called upon to beat sounds out of all kinds of unexpected objects. Sometimes new instruments have to be designed and made to produce the precise effects a composer needs.

The percussionist is the only musician to deal with noise as well as musical sounds. What is the difference? The oscillograph, which shows us the picture of soundwaves, gives the answer:

a) the uneven sound wave of an exploding rocket: *noise*

b) the repeated pattern of an organ note: *musical sound*

What makes the sound?

Percussion means 'the striking of one object with or against another'. In any percussion instrument one part is struck, either by the player's hand or *beater* (as in drums) or by another part of the instrument (as in a rattle).

Instruments of indefinite pitch
Some of these simply make a noise.
(Not drawn to scale)
Clappers
Castanets, claves, whip
Scrapers
Guiro
Rattles
Maracas, chocalho, cabaca
Drums
Bass drum, tenor drum, tom-tom, side drum, bongos, conga drum, timbales, tabor, *tambourin de Provence*
Frame drums
Tambourine without jingles

claves

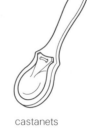

castanets

whip

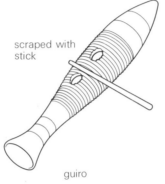

scraped with stick

guiro

(section)

buckshot rattles against shell when shaken

maracas

cabaca

Some make a complex sound, not heard as a note of definite pitch.
Slit drums
Wood block, temple block
Triangles
Cymbals
Clash, suspended, ride, hi-hat, splash
Jingles
Jingle-ring, jingling johnny
Frame drum with jingles
Tambourine
Tam-tams
Cowbells

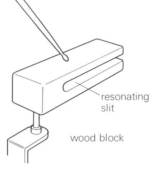

resonating slit

wood block

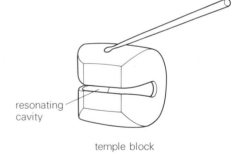

resonating cavity

temple block

single head nailed to shell

jingles

frame drum with jingles

clapper

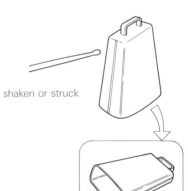

shaken or struck

cowbell

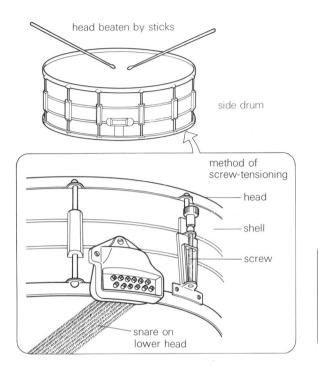

head beaten by sticks

side drum

method of
screw-tensioning

head

shell

screw

snare on
lower head

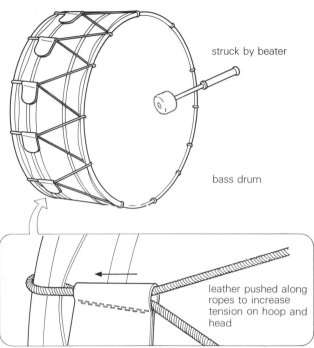

struck by beater

bass drum

leather pushed along
ropes to increase
tension on hoop and
head

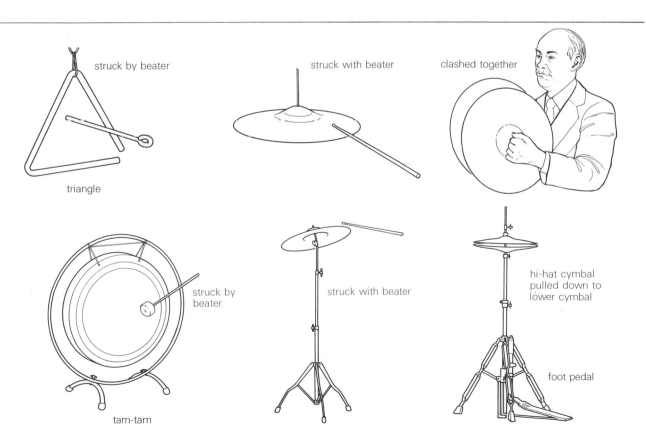

struck by beater

triangle

struck with beater

clashed together

tam-tam

struck by
beater

struck with beater

hi-hat cymbal
pulled down to
lower cymbal

foot pedal

Timpani
Drums which can be tuned to a
note of definite pitch

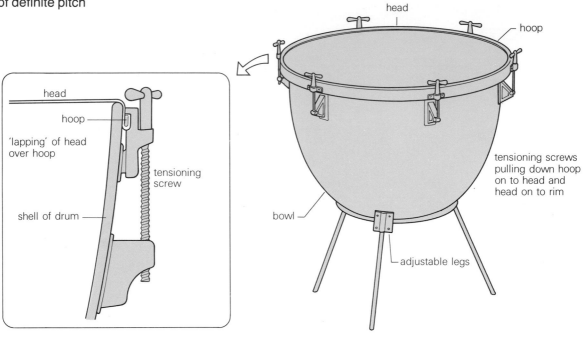

head

hoop

tensioning screws
pulling down hoop
on to head and
head on to rim

bowl

adjustable legs

head

hoop

'lapping' of head
over hoop

tensioning
screw

shell of drum

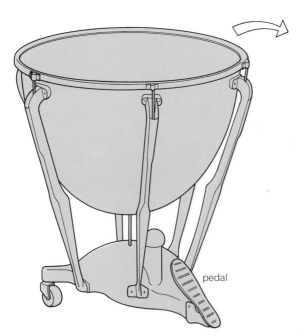

pedal

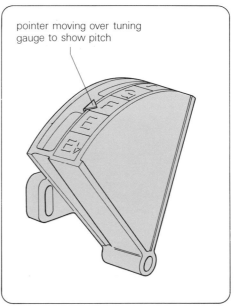

pointer moving over tuning
gauge to show pitch

Tuned percussion

These instruments play pitched notes.
(Not drawn to scale)
Xylophones
Xylophone, marimba
Metallophones
Glockenspiel, bell-lyra, vibraphone
Chimes
Tubular bells, chime bars
Antique cymbals
Tuned gongs

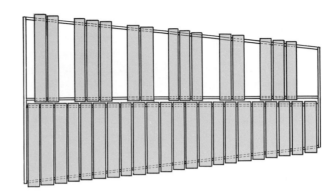

layout of notes in xylophone, glockenspiel etc.

the maker tunes a xylophone bar by shortening it if it plays too low a note, removing some of the underside if it plays too high a note

notes struck by beaters

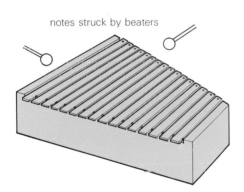

simple metallophone with resonating chamber

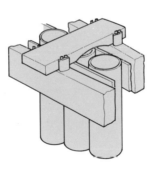

tubular resonator in xylophone

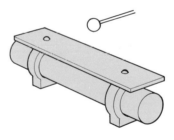

beater hits chime bar and activates sympathetic vibrations in air in hollow tube through hole

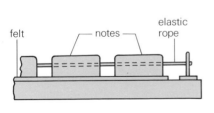

felt   notes   elastic rope

method of stringing tuned percussion notes

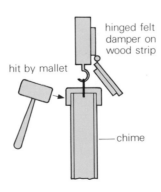

hinged felt damper on wood strip

hit by mallet

chime

section of tubular bell chime

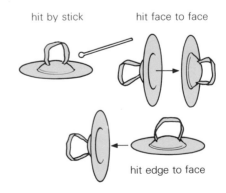

hit by stick   hit face to face

hit edge to face

three methods of playing antique cymbals

Castanets

The traditional instrument of the Spanish folk dancer, the castanets are made from the *castaña* (chestnut) tree, and consist of two pieces of wood shaped like the bowl of a spoon, held together by a cord.

The flamenco dancer holds a pair in each hand but orchestral castanets are normally fastened to a handle, shaken by one hand and struck against the other. Sometimes they are mounted for striking with a drumstick.

They are used in de Falla's *Three-cornered hat*, Bizet's *Carmen* and in non-Spanish music like Prokofiev's Piano Concerto.

Wood block

The wood block is a rectangular block of hardwood with a slit cut parallel to the long edge. When struck above the slit by a hard stick an incisive 'clop' is produced, as heard in 'Popular Song' from Walton's *Façade*.

Temple blocks (known as 'skulls') were very popular in 1920s dance music. Usually in sets of two or four different sizes, a higher or lower 'plop' is sounded depending on the size of the block. In his opera *The Knot Garden* Michael Tippett writes for five blocks.

The technical name for a wood block is a slit drum.

Some effects and how percussionists provide them

Wind machine
A slatted wooden cylinder turned at different speeds against a taut canvas sheet. (Strauss, *Don Quixote*)

Thunder sheet
A large metal sheet shaken to produce the sound of thunder. (Strauss, *Alpine Symphony*)

Chains
A large chain rattled on to a metal box or tray. (Schoenberg, *Gurrelieder*)

Coconut shells
Clapped together to make the sound of horses' hooves. (Grofé, *Grand Canyon Suite*)

Bird whistle
Egg-cup sized container, which when filled with water and blown into imitates bird song. (Haydn, *Toy Symphony*)

Tambourine

Profile
Size: average diameter 25 cm
Made of: plastic or calfskin head, wooden frame, metal jingles
Sound made by: striking head or shaking frame
First example: Egypt, about 2500 BC
Relations: timbales, jingle-ring

The Arabs forbade jingles on their tambourines as it was thought that they were like the bells believed to drive out angels. To this day Spanish tambourines often have no jingles – as in de Falla's *Master Peter's Puppet Show*.

The tambourine consists of a round hoop over which a *head* is nailed. This may be struck by the hand, knuckle or finger (sometimes the knee), or a drumstick. Around the frame are pairs of *jingles* which sound when shaken, when the head is struck or a moistened thumb rubbed around the head.

The tambourine was played by the Ancient Greeks and Romans, and was popular in Europe during the Middle Ages. One of the first composers to use it in the orchestra was Mozart who included it in his *German Dances* of 1787. In his *Nutcracker* ballet music, which has dances from many parts of the world, Tchaikovsky asks for the tambourine to be played with the thumb, struck and shaken.

The jingle-ring, a tambourine without a head, is used sometimes in the orchestra and frequently in rock bands.

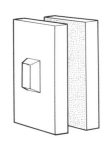

Sandpaper blocks
Rubbed together to accompany the soft shoe shuffle. (Copland, *Music for a Great City*)

Sleigh bells
Shaken strap, frame or handle carrying bells. (Elgar, *Cockaigne*: imitating horses' harness)

Ratchet
A cog lifts wood strip which falls back making click. (Strauss, *Till Eulenspiegel*)

Cow bell
Shaken (Mahler, Sixth Symphony) or hit with a drumstick. (Lambert, *Rio Grande*)

Whip
Two strong strips of wood clapped together. (Britten's *Young Person's Guide to the Orchestra*)

Triangle

Profile
Size: average 16 cm each side
Made of: steel
Sound made by: striking with beater
First example: Europe, 10th century
Relations: sistrum

Supposedly the world's biggest triangle is at the American War Cemetery, Epinal, France. Each side is 70 cm in length.

Franz Liszt gave the audience at the first performance of his Piano Concerto in E flat in 1853 a surprise: it included a solo for triangle.

The triangle was first heard in the orchestra in 1710. Its ancestor, the Egyptian sistrum, existed as long ago as 2700 BC. This was a frame carrying metal jingles which sounded when shaken. As recently as Mozart's time the triangle had jingles, but during the nineteenth century these stopped being used.

The modern instrument is, of course, triangular in shape and has one open corner. This prevents its sound being of any particular pitch, and helps give a distinctive clear 'ting' when the instrument is struck by its metal beater. It is suspended by a loop of gut or nylon passing around, or sometimes through, the bar and the sound is *damped* between the player's finger and thumb.

Beaters of varying weight are used to give different qualities of sound, including a steel knitting-needle.

Percussion instruments of Latin America

Maracas
Dried *gourds,* filled with hard seeds or shot, fastened to handles and shaken

Chilean woman playing a round frame drum with a padded stick

Bolivian pipe and tabor player

By hitting two arms of the triangle alternately on the inside, at high speed, a *roll* or *trill* can be played, heard to perfection at the beginning of 'Anitra's Dance' from Grieg's *Peer Gynt*.

Below: A trill being played by hitting two sides of the triangle from inside the angle

Below left: A triangle being hit on the outside to produce a single note

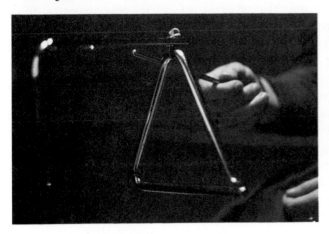

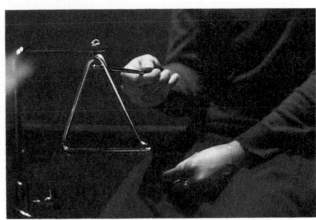

Reco-reco
A long piece of wood with carved ridges, held at the top by a handle, and scraped with a wooden stick

Cabaca
Held like *maracas* the *cabaca* has strung beads on the outside of a gourd which rattle against it. Played by shaking or striking against the palm

Mexican double-headed square frame drum called a *huasteque* and played with a stick

Cymbals

Profile
Size: up to 66 cm diameter
Made of: copper/tin alloy
Sound made by: two clashed *plates,* or plate struck by stick
First example: Asia Minor, 1200 BC
Relations: tam-tam

Clashed at the climax of many pieces of music, cymbals look as spectacular as they sound. The player brings the two round metal *plates* together, held by leather straps fastened through holes in their central domes.

Cymbalists have been demonstrating their skill for centuries, although the shapes of their instruments have varied from almost flat discs to hemispheres at different times. Like many other percussion instruments they were used in the East long before becoming known in Europe in the eighteenth century. The first symphony in which they were heard was Haydn's 'Military' Symphony of 1794.

Hitting a suspended cymbal with a drumstick was an effect introduced during the nineteenth century. A *tremolo* can be produced by using two sticks, one on each side of the cymbal.

Wire brushes instead of sticks were required by Mahler as long ago as 1895. Modern jazz drummers, of course, use numerous sizes of cymbal.

The hi-hat clashes two cymbals by means of a foot pedal. This has been an essential part of the drummer's kit since the 1920s.

The ride cymbal, 45 cm to 60 cm in diameter and specially tapered, later became equally important.

The sizzle cymbal, either with rivets vibrating in holes punched through the plate, or a light chain or thin metal strips resting on the cymbal, has been introduced more recently.

The Chinese have used cymbals of many types and sizes for centuries. They range in size from tiny pairs used by actors to the almost 100 cm-diameter cymbals in Mongolian temples. They are also used on the battlefield alongside drums.

Right: This view of drummer Billy Cobham shows how the player sees the ride cymbals, suspended at different angles, and the hi-hat, operated by the left foot.

Tam-tams and gongs

The world's most famous tam-tam is probably the monster appearing on the screen before every J Arthur Rank film. In fact, the giant wielding the beater is striking a cardboard disc, miming to a Chinese tam-tam played by the distinguished percussionist James Blades.

Using a beater with a large soft *head*, a tam-tam tremolo can start so quietly that you can't be certain if you're hearing any sound at all. But the volume can be increased gradually until it can be heard through the largest orchestra, recording equipment is damaged and listeners put their hands over their ears.

Strictly speaking, a gong gives a note of definite pitch while a tam-tam, like a cymbal, does not. Although the names tend to be used indiscriminately, tuned gongs are specifically required in several works, including Tippett's *Triple Concerto* and Boulez's *Pli Selon Pli*. Both tam-tam and gong usually consist of a narrow-rimmed bronze disc, hung from a wooden or metal frame. First used in the orchestra by Gossec in 1791, instruments of this type are particularly associated with China and nearby countries. They were known there at least 1400 years ago.

The qualities of the tam-tam are well demonstrated at the very end of 'Mars' from Holst's suite *The Planets*, where a long tremolo is followed by a single, loud stroke instilling fear in every listener. Tchaikovsky uses an isolated tam-tam note in his Sixth Symphony to achieve a similar effect.

A Burmese suspended gong

An orchestral gong being played by a member of the Royal Philharmonic Orchestra, London

Bass drum

Profile
Size: diameter up to 100 cm,
width up to 50 cm
Made of: plastic or calfskin
head; wooden shell
Sound made by: beater
striking head
First example: Sumeria,
about 2000 BC

In a marching band the bass drum gives the signal to start, provides a steady beat throughout, and gives the signal for the band to finish playing.

The bass drum became widely known in Europe in the eighteenth century, when there was a great deal of interest in Eastern customs (it originated in the East), including Turkish Janissary military bands. Gluck (1714-1787) was probably the first composer to write for bass drum in the orchestra, but Mozart's introduction of bass drum, cymbals and triangle in *Il Seraglio* (1782) gave real Eastern colour to this opera set in Turkey. The drummer was asked to play with a beater in one hand and a *Rute*, or switch of twigs, in the other.

Modern bass drums have two heads of plastic or calfskin, *tensioned* by means of *rods*. (Some regimental bands still use rope-tensioned drums which are not so heavy.) Players choose from a range of sticks of different weights and types of head to make the required sound. Although the drum heads are tensioned so that a note of definite pitch is avoided, the bass drum can produce a surprisingly wide range of sounds.

Hear any funeral march and you will feel the bass drum's awesome, unreverberant 'thunk'. It plays the part of cannon in Tchaikovsky's *1812 Overture,* and in the 'Dies Irae' of Verdi's *Requiem* there is a string of solo notes for bass drum, played on the largest available. This part is unusual for another reason, too. The notes are played not on the heavy, accented beats of the bar but on the lighter 'off' beats.

Above: The bass drummer of the Scots Guards marching between several snare drummers

Right: An orchestral percussionist plays a roll on a bass drum mounted on a swivel stand

In his Tenth Symphony Mahler includes two isolated strokes on muffled bass drum, inspired by part of a fireman's funeral cortège he witnessed in New York.

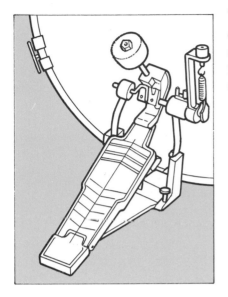

Until the 1960s the bass drum in dance music and jazz always emphasised the heavy beats, the drummer playing the bass drum by means of a foot-pedal, leaving the hands free for the rest of the 'kit'. Nowadays, in both jazz and rock, the bass drum plays a much freer and more interesting part.

Left: Close-up of a bass drum foot pedal. Pressing the pedal causes the beater to hit the drum. When the foot is lifted, the beater returns to its original position by means of the spring on the right.

In 1928 Gene Krupa became the first to play bass drum on a jazz record. Previously American recording companies prohibited its use owing to its effect on their recording equipment.

Tenor drum

The tenor drum is a deeper type of side drum, without snare.

It may be played with hard or soft sticks, and has been requested by a number of twentieth-century composers, including Milhaud (*Suite Provençale*) and Stravinsky (*The Soldier's Tale*). The one on the right is being played in Andrzej Panufnik's *Nocturne*.

Tom-tom

Inspired by African drums, the modern tom-tom has a single head, without a snare.

There are normally at least two in a drum kit, the smaller often fastened to the bass drum and the larger sizes standing on legs. They are not tuned to precise notes, but the difference in size gives sounds of higher or lower pitch.

Composers Malcolm Arnold and John Cage are amongst those who have written for tom-tom. In Latin-American music single-headed, open-ended drums like these are called timbales.

Side drum

Profile
Size: 35-38 cm in diameter,
12-20 cm deep
Made of: plastic or calfskin
head; wood or metal shell;
gut, nylon, wire or wire-
covered silk snare
First example: France, by
1575
Sound made by: stick
striking head
Relations: tabor, tenor drum.

The tabor, widespread in medieval Europe, appeared in many shapes and sizes. It always had a *snare* on the head that was actually struck (the *batter-head*). By the sixteenth century tabors existed which were worn at the player's side and their snares were on the lower head. These were the first side drums, important military instruments used to convey commands to the troops.

The side drum was found occasionally in opera scores during the eighteenth century and was finally established as a member of the orchestra by Rossini (1792-1868). Two solo side drum rolls begin the overture to his *La Gazza Ladra,* and there are numerous other instances of its capabilities in his other works. The Danish composer Carl Nielsen (1865-1931) was a more recent devotee: in his Clarinet Concerto it plays a duet with the soloist, while the side drummer makes a prominent and partly improvised contribution to the Fifth Symphony.

The snare is important, and the side drum is often in fact called the 'snare drum'. The device was known as long ago as the time of the Crusades, when it was also sometimes found on tambourines. By the seventeenth century there was a mechanism allowing the snare tension to be adjusted. This ensures that the crisp sound is heard immediately the stick strikes the batter-head. (The snares actually double the number of vibrations made by the head.) In modern drums a lever instantly throws the snares out of operation when required.

Modern orchestral side drum, showing snare and snare release

This military side drum uses ropes to adjust the tension of the heads. The snare can just be seen on the lower head of drum in the background.

The two alternative ways of holding side drum sticks:

'traditional' grip

'matched' grip

In Ravel's *Bolero* the side drum begins the whole work. Its solo phrase is repeated 165 times, each slightly louder than the time before. It plays throughout the piece until the last two bars: about 14 minutes in all.

Traditionally the side drum is played with a pair of wooden sticks. The player can produce a long and even roll, conventionally by two strokes of the left, then two strokes of the right stick (called 'Daddy-Mammy'). The flam, drag and paradiddle are some of the names for the other side drum strokes. The rim-shot is produced by the sticks striking the rim of the drum and its head at the same time.

Wire brushes are frequently used in place of sticks in jazz, giving a rhythmic yet inconspicuous backing for the band — the hallmarks of the good jazz drummer.

Tabor

The tabor, known in Roman times, was popular throughout Europe in the Middle Ages. The large tabor was the ancestor of the modern side drum and the smaller size was used in combination with the pipe.

The *tambourin de Provence* is sometimes used in orchestral music. Its diameter is less than its depth and there is a single snare over the batter-head, as in all tabors. Bizet included this folk-like drum in the 'Farandole' of his *L'Arlésienne,* and it is still used for dance accompaniment in parts of France and Spain.

Flemish tabor player of 1581, drummer to Guild of Archers

The domestic washboard was played by folk blues singers using thimbles on their fingers. It was widely heard during the skiffle craze of the 1950s.

Often, as in this picture of a July 4th picnic band, the washboard had other home-made percussion instruments added to it. As well as two small frying pans, this player has fixed two cymbals to his board, making a full percussion 'kit'. He is playing a kazoo at the same time!

Timpani

Profile
Size: 48-78 cm diameter
Made of: plastic or calfskin head; fibreglass or copper bowl
Sound made by: stick striking head
First example: Persia, by 600 AD
Relations: nakers

The nakers, ancestors of the timpani, in present-day Tunisia

In Variation 13 of Elgar's *Enigma Variations* a timpani roll gives the impression of a ship's engines. Players always use two coins for this effect instead of sticks.

At the base of the timpani *bowl* is a small hole which allows the air under pressure to escape. Without this the head might split when a loud note is struck.

Sitting with, yet apart from, the members of the orchestra's percussion section, the timpanist produces precisely-pitched notes from an impressive array of kettledrums. It is every percussionist's ambition to play 'timps', taking part in Classical symphonies by Mozart and Haydn as well as the works of more recent composers.

Since the timpani or kettledrums can be accurately tuned to notes of particular pitch they contribute to the harmonies as well as the rhythms of music.

Drums of this type existed in Persia 1400 years ago. The smaller sizes (known as nakers), are still played all over the Middle East. The larger sizes were introduced to the West in the fifteenth century, pairs of hemispherical drums mounted on a camel or horse while played. They inspired European cavalry kettledrums, first used in the orchestra in the seventeenth century. There they have remained ever since, although of course, their tuning mechanism has been greatly improved.

Until the early sixteenth century the drums were tensioned by rope, but by 1550 screw-tensioning was in use. Machine timpani appeared only in the nineteenth century (450 years after they had been suggested by Leonardo da Vinci). There are various types of mechanisms, but they have one feature in common: instantaneous change of pitch by the operation of a foot-pedal or handle. They also make a *glissando* possible by changing the tension immediately after striking the head.

Orchestral timpanist with the BBC Symphony Orchestra

Two timpani were normal in the orchestra until the nineteenth century. Since then there have usually been three, although four or five are often required and Berlioz called for sixteen in his *Grande messe des morts*. Generally associated with loud passages of music they can also be used to create a mood of tranquillity as at the very opening of Beethoven's Violin Concerto.

The bowls, previously of copper, are now often fibreglass. Heads, once always calfskin, are now usually plastic (polyethylene terephthalate), reducing the problems caused by extremes of temperature and humidity. A range of sticks is used, often chosen by the individual player to suit particular passages of music: soft for the solo roll at the beginning of Haydn's 'Drum Roll' Symphony (no. 103), hard for the solos in Stravinsky's *Petrouchka*.

In their early days in the orchestra pairs of kettledrums were often tuned so that the larger drum played a note four lower than the smaller. This was adequate for the relatively simple harmony in most music of the time. Modern composers (notably Benjamin Britten) don't hesitate to write actual melodies for their timpani.

Why does the timpanist lean heavily on the instruments? This is to 'settle' the head after slackening the *vellum* to tune down to a lower note. This prevents the pitch from dropping abruptly when the head is struck.

Normal grip for timpani sticks, demonstrated by James Blades

Why does the timpanist whisper to the drums? It is not whispering. The player hums notes to check that the drum is tuned properly. When it is in tune, it responds to the hummed note.

The timpani in this picture are mounted on drum horse Claudius of the Blues and Royals in the English Household Cavalry. The drums have a shallower shell than usual, but are still a heavy weight for the horse to carry.

Xylophone

How would you show in music the dance of a skeleton? The French composer Saint-Saëns used a tune on the xylophone in his *Danse macabre*, written in 1874. The sound made by wooden beaters on its strips of wood of different lengths has a strange, dry, chippy quality.

The xylophone was one of the first instruments ever used for playing melodies, probably in prehistoric Africa and Asia. It is still used today in various forms by musicians all over the world.

By the sixteenth century it had arrived in Europe, although it was to be another 300 years before it appeared in the orchestra.

The modern xylophone provides up to 48 notes, each supported on felt above a tube *resonator*. The notes are laid out like a piano keyboard, with the 'black notes' behind the 'white notes'. Beaters with wooden, rubber, felt and other types of head are used.

In this century composers have often written very complicated parts for the xylophone, such as that in Messiaen's *Chronochromie*. There are even pieces for solo xylophone.

The xylophone can also be heard in concerts by bands and light orchestra. The player normally has two beaters in each hand. The American jazzman Red Norvo was an acknowledged virtuoso performer.

Modern orchestral xylophone

In 1931 the American Clair Omar Musser had a super-xylophone made. It was 3 m long and weighed 635 kg.

African xylophones played by Bwaba musicians in Upper Volta. These instruments have between 12 and 21 wooden bars. Beneath each one is a resonator made from a hollowed-out gourd which has been dried and varnished. One of these is visible under the note at the nearest end of the instrument.

Marimba

Profile

Made of: wooden bars

Sound made by: beater
striking bar

First example: ?Africa date
unknown

Relations: xylophone, claves

The marimba is a type of large xylophone, its deepest note sounding an octave below the lowest on the xylophone.

Its *bars* are also made of wood, but since they are not so deep as those of the xylophone and softer beaters are used there is a noticeable difference in sound between the two instruments. This is emphasised by the resonator beneath each bar.

In addition to being heard in works by Copland, Malcolm Arnold and others there are concertos for marimba and orchestra by Milhaud and Creston.

Marimbas are particularly important in the music of Central America. In marimba bands there are sometimes two or three players to each instrument.

Marimba de tecomates, a popular Guatemalan folk instrument

Exhibited in Keswick, Cumbria, are several *rock harmonicas.* These are large xylophones, the notes made of slabs of stone found locally. (Strictly they should be called lithophones, as *xylo* means 'made from wood' and *litho* means 'from stone'.) The one in the picture, which took the Richardson family 13 years to make, has a range of 5 octaves. Its highest note is made by a slab of stone 15 cm long and its lowest by one 93 cm long. The Richardsons gave a performance on their rock harmonica in front of Queen Victoria.

Glockenspiel

Profile
Size: various
Made of: steel bars
Sound made by: mallet striking bar
First example: ?Germany, eighteenth century
Relations: xylophone, vibraphone

The metal bars of the glockenspiel give the sound of little bells, perfect for adding a delightfully apt daintiness to the 'Waltz' from Tchaikovsky's *Sleeping Beauty* and 'Dance of the Hours' from Ponchielli's *La Gioconda*.

Laid on felt, the bars are arranged like those of the xylophone but without resonators. Mallets with hard ends, sometimes even metal, are used. Most glockenspiels have a range of 30 or 37 notes.

Metallophones – xylophone-type instruments in which the notes are produced by metal rather than wood – were known in the Far East more than 1000 years ago.

Left: The bell-lyra, used in many marching bands, has a very penetrating tone. It is played vertically.

A glockenspiel player in the BBC Symphony Orchestra.

Profile
Size: 5-10 cm diameter
Made of: bronze
Sound made by: striking edge to edge, edge to face, or striking with beater
First example: Greece, about 500 BC
Relations: castanets, glockenspiel

Antique cymbals

Sometimes called 'crotales', these small cymbal-shaped metal instruments often give notes of an actual pitch.

In Ancient Greece they were probably played by dancing girls. The girls also used tiny 'finger-cymbals' fastened to the thumb and forefinger and played like castanets, by snapping thumb and finger together.

A set of crotales from 5 cm to 41 cm in diameter survived in the ruins of the Roman city, Pompeii.

In 1839 Berlioz introduced crotales to the orchestra in *Romeo and Juliet*. Their other-world, other-time quality attracted many French composers and they are heard to great effect in Ravel's *Daphnis and Chloe* and Debussy's *L'après-midi d'un faune*.

Antique cymbals are now available in sets giving all the notes of the chromatic octave. Jazz-rock musician Mike Gibbs has used them to add their exotic tinkle to mysterious chords.

Vibraphone

Profile
Made of: metal alloy bars
each approx 3 cm wide
Sound made by: beater
striking bar, and
mechanically-pulsed
resonator
First example: USA, 1916
Relations: glockenspiel,
xylophone

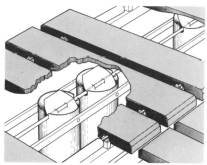

Diagram showing revolving discs
at the upper end of the
vibraphone's resonators

Profile
Made of: brass or steel
tubes of varying height
Sound made by: striking
with mallet
First example: England,
1855
Relations: bells,
glockenspiel

Right: This player with London's
Royal Philharmonic Orchestra is
using two mallets at the same time
to move quickly from one tube to
another. The upper mallet shows
clearly the angle at which it must
strike the cap of the bell to
produce the best tone.

The distinctive sounds of the vibraphone, or vibraharp, result from the harnessing of an electric motor to a glockenspiel with resonators to fulfil the demands of early twentieth-century 'novelty soloists'.

Beneath each bar of the vibraphone is a resonator, as in the marimba, closed at the lower end. A revolving disc, driven by the motor, alternately closes and opens the upper end, producing the unique throbbing tone. By means of a foot-operated mechanism the player is able to sustain notes just as a pianist does with a sustaining pedal. Rubber-cored soft-headed beaters are normally used.

The vibraphone is heard in Britten's *Spring Symphony* and Vaughan Williams' Eighth Symphony, but it is also an important jazz instrument. Lionel Hampton's many recordings have delighted listeners since the 1930s. Milt Jackson's 'vibes', with discs set to rotate at a slower speed than normal, made a distinctive contribution to the Modern Jazz Quartet during the 1950s. More recently Gary Burton, adept with four or five *hammers* simultaneously, has greatly expanded the instrument's scope.

Tubular bells

As substitute church bells the tubular bells (sometimes called 'chimes') have the advantage of being much easier to take from one concert hall to another!

A set may contain up to 20 tubes, hanging from a frame. There is a cap over the upper end of each tube (the lower end is open) which is struck by a rawhide *mallet*. The chimes can usually be damped by a felt-covered flap operated by the player's hand or foot.

Some percussion groups

The steel band

Complete bands of oil drums (pans) originated in Trinidad. There are four sizes of pan: treble (ping pong), alto (guitar pan), tenor (cello pan) and bass (boom). From four to thirty-two notes can be obtained from the skilfully-worked pan, in which different-sized flat areas are beaten out on the drum base. Painted lines surround the area of each note, struck by rubber-ended beaters. All types of music are played by these bands of attractively mellow-toned drums.

Junior percussion band

Many children begin to play percussion at school. In addition to full-size or slightly smaller versions of instruments used in other bands and orchestras, special instruments are available which help to make things more fun. These include chime bars, metallophones and many sizes of tom-tom.

The gamelan

The sounds of the gamelan, the orchestra of Indonesia, made a deep and lasting impression on many Western composers, including Debussy, Puccini, Britten and Messiaen. Virtually all the orchestra consists of percussion. Various gongs, xylophones, drums and bamboo rattles give exotic and delicately-coloured effects. In 1980 an English Gamelan Orchestra was formed in London. The picture shows a women's gamelan orchestra in Jakarta.

Drum kit

A typical drum kit, played by the drummer in the rock band *Status Quo*

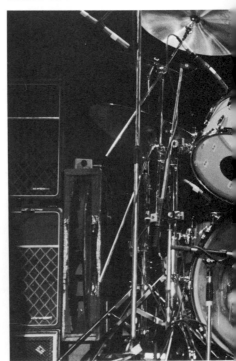

Percussion terms

acorn: swelling at tip of side drum stick

bar: note of xylophone, glockenspiel, hit by beater

batter-head: head which is struck

beater: implement for striking percussion instrument

bowl: shell of timpani with rim over which head is stretched

brush: wire-bristled brush used in side drum and cymbal playing

cross-over beating: crossing one hand over the other in timpani playing

damp: to cut short sounds produced by instrument by (in drums) resting a felt pad or folded duster on the head, (in cymbals) by touching or holding the plate, using the fingers or convenient clothing

double-headed: drum with two heads

glissando: slide in pitch made on tuned percussion by sliding beater along bars and on timpani by releasing tension immediately after striking the head

gourd: hard-shelled fruit used in construction of various Latin-American instruments

hammer: hammer-shaped beater used on xylophone, marimba or vibraphone; carpenter's hammer used to play anvil

head: plastic or skin part of drum normally beaten, or end of beater used to strike instrument as opposed to the held end

jingle: pair of small cymbals clashed when tambourine, into which they are set, is shaken; small metal spheres containing shot rattled in sleigh bells etc

key: T-shaped device temporarily fitted over top of some tuning screws

kit: percussion instruments conveniently assembled for one player especially in jazz, rock or dance band

lapping: securing of drum head to hoop

let ring: instruction not to damp note

mallet: beater for glockenspiel, vibraphone or tubular bells

matched grip: method of holding sticks with similar grip in each hand — traditional for timpani sticks and now often used also for side drum sticks

plate: metal part of cymbal

rabbit grip: method of holding left-hand side drum stick in unmatched grip

resonator: hollow body containing air amplifying vibrations of struck surface

rim: edge of drum shell or timpani body

rod: threaded rod tensioning drum head(s)

roll: repeated strokes with one or two beaters or sticks

screw-tension: controlling the tightness of head by means of threaded rods

shell: the wooden or metal part of a drum

single-headed: drum with one head

sling: rope or strap allowing drum to be worn by player during performance

snare: wires lying against lower head of side drum or upper head of tabor vibrating when batter-head is struck

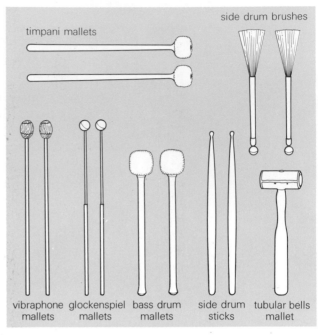

timpani mallets

side drum brushes

vibraphone mallets · glockenspiel mallets · bass drum mallets · side drum sticks · tubular bells mallet

stick: form of beater, especially for drum

suspend: to hang an instrument so that it can be played conveniently

tension: even stretching of head to produce desired tone quality or pitch

thumb roll: roll on tambourine made by rubbing moistened thumb round head

traps: percussion instruments, particularly in the theatre and especially the smaller items, from the nineteenth-century term trappings

tremolo: roll, especially on bass drum, cymbals and gong

trill: roll, especially on triangle

tuning screws: threaded rods tensioning timpani head

unmatched grip: traditional method of holding side drum sticks, with rabbit grip for left hand stick

vellum: skin (usually calfskin) head

Keyboard instruments

1 pipe organ
2 grand piano
3 upright piano
4 harpsichord
5 clavichord
6 celeste

Most people who play a musical instrument can perform on the piano – or at least get a tune from one. Many learn the piano and then go on to other types of instrument; others pick it up on their own, as it's easy to make a sound on a piano though hard to play well. The ability to play the piano can introduce a whole family of other keyboard instruments.

There are the vast sound-worlds of the organ, the drawing room tones of the harpsichord or the quiet celeste and clavichord, not to mention the new sounds of electronic keyboard instruments.

Keyboard instruments such as the piano and organ are perhaps the most satisfying to play as solo instruments. This is because a keyboard, and sometimes also pedals, enable each finger and foot to sound a different note, so keyboard performers can produce chords, play several melodies at once or play a tune with an accompaniment. Sometimes two players play duets on one or more pianos.

How keyboards developed

The picture above, which comes from a 13th-century psalter, shows King David playing an organ with separate levers for each pipe. The man on the right is pumping bellows with his feet, and in front is a hurdy-gurdy.

A keyboard allows the fingers to operate mechanisms that produce sounds. The feet can be used on some types of instruments to work a pedal-board which does the same. Sometimes, as in the piano, the player can vary the tone or volume of the sounds by controlling the pressure and speed of the fingers. But with instruments like the organ, the player's fingers only switch the sounds on or off and cannot control them in the same way.

The beginnings of keyboard instruments go back to about 250 BC, and a Greek organ called the hydraulis. The keyboard of the hydraulis consisted of hand-operated levers or keys, each as far apart as the organ pipes – much too wide for the player to control several notes at once with the fingers. This continued to be the design of keyboards until about the thirteenth century. These instruments could only have produced slow and simple music.

Then better ways of connecting keys to pipes were invented, allowing the keys to be placed closer together. But even these early keyboards were very simple, with fewer notes than the organs of today. By 1400, the keyboard had achieved its present arrangement of black and white keys producing notes a semitone apart. The keys were further narrowed to permit faster playing and easier production of chords. Organs and harpsichords were then built with two or more keyboards, each producing a different tone quality. The range of notes they could play, both high and low, increased, culminating in a seven-octave range for the piano by 1900.

Instrument makers have added keyboards to many kinds of instruments, particularly wind and string. These include the autoharp (a kind of keyboard zither), and free-reed instruments such as the melodica (a keyboard mouth organ) or the accordion and concertina, which are portable bellows organs.

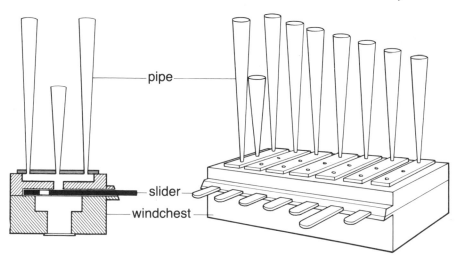

pipe

slider

windchest

This diagram of an 11th-century organ shows how each pipe (or group of three pipes) had its own key or 'slider'. These were pulled out to allow the notes to sound.

Most keyboard music can be played by hands with a width of one octave (C to C), but Chopin (seen above) had large hands which enabled him to span a tenth (C to E) easily, and his music sometimes requires hands of this size. Rachmaninov had huge hands that could span a twelfth (C to G), and his left hand could play a chord consisting, from the bass upwards, of the notes C, Eb, G, C and G.

Right: The complicated Janko keyboard, which never successfully replaced the conventional keyboard

Below: The regular arrangement of notes within each octave, in the standard keyboard

The earliest known keyboard music is the Robertsbridge Codex, which dates from about 1320. It contains dances composed for the keyboard and keyboard arrangements of vocal music. The manuscript does not say for which instrument the music is intended but its complexity shows that it must have been a keyboard instrument with all the sharps and flats, probably an organ of some kind.

Experimental keyboards

Inventors have continually devised new kinds of keyboards in an effort to make keyboard instruments easier to play. Some of the more unusual examples which did not catch on include instruments containing a separate keyboard for the left hand in which the treble and bass are reversed, so that both hands can play passages with the same fingering. Borrowing the principle of transposing from brass and woodwind instruments, there have also been special arrangements of keys that enable a performer to use the same fingering for the same music in different keys. However, none of these new keyboards has ever been widely used, and most keyboard music now played is written for the standard keyboard.

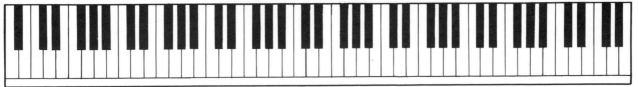

How a pipe organ works

An early description of the organ or 'organum' was written by St Augustine. Although the word was used to describe all musical instruments he refers especially to an instrument of 'many pipes blown with bellows'.

There are three main parts of an organ: the pump and windchest, the pipes, and the keyboard and valves which admit wind to the pipes. The pump fills the windchest with air under pressure, and pressing a key allows air into a particular pipe or set of pipes, producing a sound.

The pump and windchest

In early organs, sets of bellows were used to create wind pressure. These pumped air into a windchest, and sliders or valves were used to release air from the chest to the pipes. In the first organ, Ctesibius' hydraulis of 250 BC, once air had been pumped in by hand, a water cistern was used to keep the air under pressure. Water continued to be used, along with different types of bellows, as a means of maintaining wind pressure, until about 1890, when electric fans were used to feed wind reservoirs.

Below: Medieval organ bellows were pumped by a hand lever.

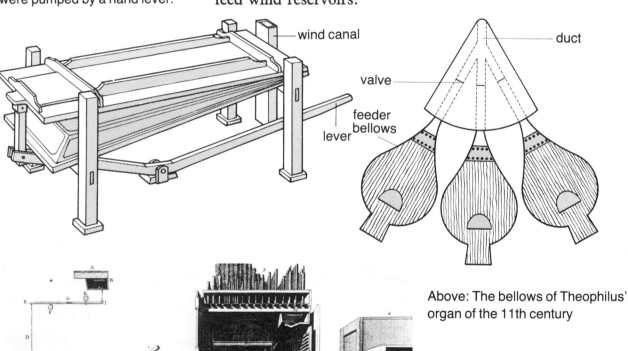

wind canal

duct

valve

feeder bellows

lever

Above: The bellows of Theophilus' organ of the 11th century

The cross-section on the left shows the bellows, the windchest and pipes, and the keyboard of an 18th-century French organ.

The pipes

A modern pipe organ contains the three basic kinds of pipes shown on this page.

The length of the pipe determines the pitch of the note, although other factors can affect this. If the top of the pipe is closed or stopped it lowers the pitch, and changes the sound quality. As with woodwind or brass instruments, the *bore* of the pipe affects its tone, and pipes vary from being almost cylindrical to conical.

The keyboard

Keyboards on organs are known as manuals, and each manual operates different groups of pipes, each group being controlled by a *stop*. The pressing of a key opens the holes in the windchest which allow a group of pipes to sound the note indicated by the key. The key is linked to the holes by *trackers* which can be mechanically or electronically operated.

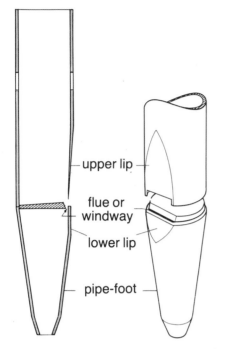

- upper lip
- flue or windway
- lower lip
- pipe-foot

Flue pipes produce a sound in much the same way as a recorder. Air is blown against the *lip* of a hole in the pipe, causing the air column in the pipe to sound.

Below: A simplified view of an organ key opening a *pallet* in the windchest and feeding air to a rank of pipes

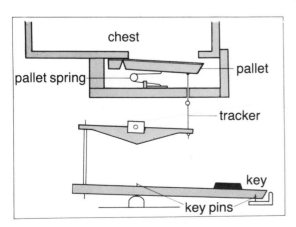

- chest
- pallet spring
- pallet
- tracker
- key
- key pins

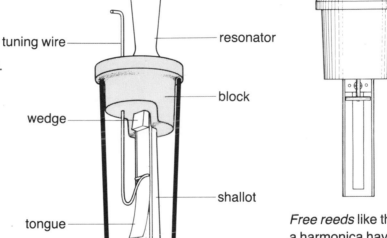

- tuning wire
- resonator
- block
- wedge
- shallot
- tongue
- boot

Free reeds like those of a harmonica have an oblong brass plate perforated with a narrow aperture through which vibrates a close-fitting brass tongue. This causes the air column in the pipe to vibrate.

Reed pipes work in a similar way to a single-reed instrument like the clarinet. Air blown through the *bore* of the pipe forces a thin brass reed to vibrate against a shallot which is rather like a woodwind mouthpiece.

Early pipe organs

Profile
First example: 250 BC
Made of: wood or metal
pipes; brass cistern;
decorated wood casing
Size: 165–186 cm high,
90 cm diameter
Four ranks of up to 18 pipes

Hydraulis

Philo of Byzantium, writing late in the third century BC, tells us how the great engineer Ctesibius invented a 'syrinx played by the hands'. This was the hydraulis, in which air was pumped into an upturned funnel, immersed in water. The surrounding water kept the air at high pressure, so that it continued to flow steadily to the pipes if the pump faltered or even stopped for a while. The player pressed keys that pulled out sliders beneath the pipes. These sliders contained holes which let air into the pipes. Each slider could have several holes and sound a set of pipes together.

The Hydraulis

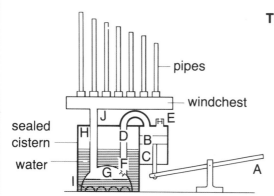

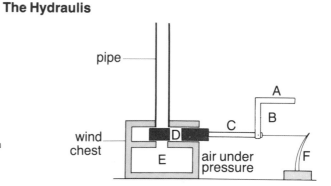

Wind-producing mechanism. Pump A moves plunger B in cylinder C, forcing air through pipe D to upturned funnel G. Non-return valves E and F allow air in, but not out. Apertures I let water into cistern H, forcing air through pipe J to the pipes.

Key and slider mechanism. Key A crosses pivot B to push slider C, until hole D lets wind out of windchest E to the pipe.

The hydraulis continued to be used for several hundred years, and was played mainly at public events such as circuses, theatres and chariot races.

A roman mosaic showing a hydraulis and a cornu player

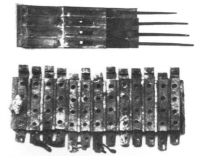

Parts of a Roman organ were found in Hungary, and reconstructed in 1959. Scholars think leather bellows were used in place of the cistern of the hydraulis.

Theophilus' Organ

In the eleventh century, the monk Theophilus wrote an encyclopedia on making church objects which gave instructions on building a two-octave organ. It had thin copper flue pipes of equal diameter, and these were soldered and their tone 'voiced' by adjusting the mouths.

His work is important for it tells us that by this time – between the ninth and eleventh centuries – the organ had become commonplace in churches. Large bellows were used, and everything was set for the fourteenth-century invention of the *rollerboard*, to take the key action sideways, so that a great many more pipes could be played from one keyboard. The bigger organs were *great* organs, fixed in churches, each set of pipes giving the *unison*, fifth and octave of a note, to produce the full organ sound known as a diapason.

Positive Organ

With a *chromatic keyboard* of two octaves, and a pair of bellows operated by a second person, the positive organ was a large, but portable organ. It had a complete rank of pipes, in two rows, often with extra bass pipes. Positive organs were frequently built into larger church organs and operated by a separate manual.

Portative Organ

Smaller than the positive organ, and better for everyday music making, the portative was supported by a strap over the player's shoulders, with bellows pumped by the left hand, and keys or buttons played with the right. They were used from the fourteenth to sixteenth centuries.

Above: Positive organ being played in Van Eyck's 'Adoration of the Lamb', painted in 1432 for a cathedral in Ghent, Belgium. Other angels are holding a harp and a kind of violin or rebec.

Far right: Portative organ painted by Hans Memling in the second half of the fifteenth century, which has *chromatic* keys.

Right: Positive organ with woman operating bellows

Modern pipe organ

The huge pipe organs in use today began to develop from about 1400. The ranks of pipes had already been divided into two groups – *great* and *positive*, played by separate keyboards – and pedals had been added for the feet. At first the pedals merely pulled down the lower keys on the keyboard, but they were soon provided with an independent set of pipes.

Organ builders sought even greater variety and developed *stops* to enable each keyboard to produce a wider range of sounds. All modern organs have stops which are panels of buttons or switches above and to each side of the keyboards. Pulling out a stop directs the flow of air into a certain combination of pipes which gives a particular sound. The stops are named after the sounds they control, and as pipes often imitate the sounds of other instruments, the stops can have such names as flute or trumpet. Sometimes they can have names of more obscure instruments such as the soft-toned viola d'amore.

Stops also control the pitch of a note, so that the organist can change register, producing notes an octave or two octaves above or below while pressing a single key. These ranges are marked in feet (′) according to the length of pipes. The 8′ stop is the normal range. The 16′ and 32′ stops give sounds one octave or two octaves deeper, while the 4′ and 2′ stops give sounds one or two octaves higher. Intermediate stops give a fifth above or fourth below and many organs have 'mixture' stops. The stops for each keyboard can be used in any combination and 'couplers' link stops from one keyboard to another.

Many modern organs have a swell box, invented in Spain in the late seventeenth century. Pipes are enclosed in the swell box, which contains shutters that may be opened by pressing a pedal, causing the sound to get suddenly louder.

Aristide Cavaillé-Coll was one of the main creators of the 19th-century French romantic organ. Born in 1811, he had built nearly 500 organs before his death in 1899. His instruments helped to inspire music by Liszt, Saint-Saëns, Franck and Widor.

Part of an organ's pipework, showing how the pipes contrast in size

Some organs have as many as five manuals. These manuals, from the bottom upwards, operate the 'choir' organ, which has a soft and delicate sound; the great organ, which is the main and most powerful organ; the swell organ; the solo organ, with stops suitable for solo melodies; and the echo organ, which has very soft stops that can give echo effects. Most modern organs have two or three manuals (great, swell and choir) and a pedalboard, each with a wide range of stops.

Organ music

The modern organ developed mainly in northern Germany in the fifteenth and sixteenth centuries. The music of that time was polyphonic, with interweaving melodic lines producing complex forms such as the fugue. These lines can be heard best if each has a different tone colour, so the organ developed its wide range of sounds to express this music fully, for example, in the music of J S Bach (1685–1750). From about 1750 onwards the organ was less important, until its revival in France in the middle of the nineteenth century. Then, organ builders constructed instruments capable of many orchestral effects, and the keyboard virtuoso and composer Liszt popularized a style of romantic organ music. This developed into a highly expressive organ music of symphonic grandeur in the work of Saint-Saëns and Franck. Contemporary composers have exploited unusual sound combinations, sometimes requiring several players to perform pieces on one instrument.

The organist Jennifer Bate, with her feet operating the pedalboard. The pedal stops can be seen just above the pedals.

Below: The five-manual console of the organ in St Paul's Cathedral, London, made by N P Mander Ltd

Reed organs

Reed organs are organs that do not contain pipes. Instead, the keys direct air to blow over a free reed, in this case a flexible tongue of metal fixed to a frame at one end. The reed vibrates, giving out a note. The pitch depends on the length and thickness of the reed.

In the late eighteenth century, travellers brought the first mouth organs to Europe from China. These contained free reeds, which produce a note without any pipe at all. Organ builders took up free reeds with great enthusiasm, both as a source of new sounds and as a way of making smaller organs without pipes.

In 1810 Johann Casper Schlimbach produced a keyboard-operated jew's harp with knee-operated bellows, called an 'aeoline'. Anton Haeckl built a table-sized regal in 1818 called a 'physharmonika', and other free-reed organs, built in places as diverse as Berlin, Vienna, Paris and Stuttgart, were known as 'poikilorgues', 'aeolodikas' and 'orgues expressifs'.

These efforts culminated in the harmonium, which was invented by Alexandre Debain in about 1840.

The first reed organs were called regals. Small portable organs with bellows, they were invented in the 15th century. The pitch of the notes was mainly determined by the reeds, although they also had short pipes which helped to produce the notes by resonating.

The pedal bellows of the reed organ are operated alternately by the player's feet.

Right: This reed organ looks very similar to a harmonium. It has a heavy and ornate case, with a row of stops above the keyboard.

Harmonium

The harmonium is powered by bellows that are worked by two pedals, or treadles, pushed alternately to and fro, though modern instruments have electric blowers instead. The bellows force air into a windchest, and the action of the keys opens pallet holes to admit the air to the reeds. In many instruments, the bellows suck air through the reeds instead of blowing them. Stops above the keyboard allow different sets of reeds to sound, thereby varying the tone of the instrument. An ingenious percussion stop causes a small hammer to strike the reeds as they sound, making the note start quickly and enabling staccato notes, trills and fast passages to be played. Pressing the pedals harder can increase the volume, but some instruments have a knee lever that varies the volume – sometimes with two levers to control the treble and bass separately.

The harmonium became very popular in the late nineteenth and early twentieth centuries as a substitute for the pipe organ, although it declined from about 1930, superseded by the accordion (really a portable harmonium) and the electric organ. Several composers have written music specifically for it, notably Kurt Weill in *The Threepenny Opera*. It also fascinated the Viennese composers Schoenberg and Berg. Schoenberg adapted works by Busoni for the instrument, and arranged waltzes by Johann Strauss for 'salon orchestra' in which Berg played the harmonium.

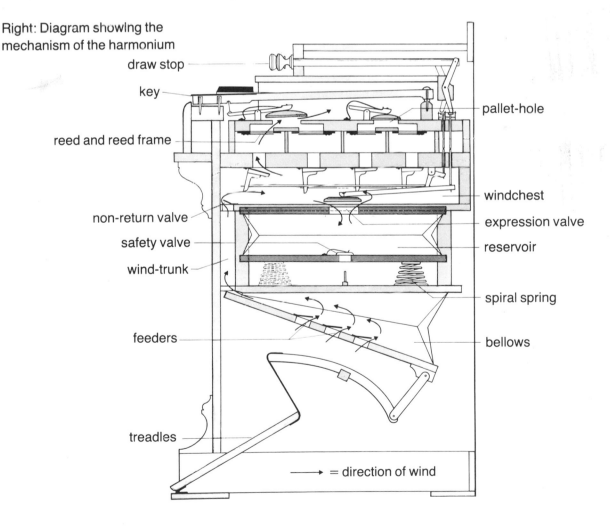

Right: Diagram showing the mechanism of the harmonium

draw stop

key

reed and reed frame

pallet-hole

windchest

non-return valve

expression valve

safety valve

reservoir

wind-trunk

spiral spring

feeders

bellows

treadles

⟶ = direction of wind

Early string keyboard instruments

Profile: Clavichord
First example: 1400
Made of: wooden case, ivory keys, brass tangents, metal strings
Compass: 3–5 octaves
Length: 80–132 cm

In this 16th-century painting the clavichord mechanism is clearly shown, the bass hammers being curved to align with the strings.

Below: The mechanism of a fretted clavichord, showing the keys which produce B and C

Organs, with pipes or reeds, make up one of the two main families of keyboard instruments. In the other, a keyboard causes a taut string to sound. This is done in two ways: by plucking the string with a *quill* carried by a *jack*, or by striking the string with a *tangent* or *hammer*.

Clavichord

In the middle ages a simple instrument called the monochord was used for teaching music theory. A single taut string rested on two bridges, one fixed and one moveable, and moving the second bridge along the string produced different pitches, as the length free to vibrate was altered.

The first clavichords were basically sets of monochords. The keys operated brass wedges called tangents that struck taut strings, causing them to sound. Each key had to be held down for the length of time a note was to sound so that the tangent remained in contact with the string, forming a bridge. The pitch of the note depended on the position of the tangent along the string. The length of string from tuning pin to tangent was free to vibrate, the string on the other side of the tangent being 'damped' by a piece of cloth.

At first there were more keys than strings; each string had several keys and could produce different notes depending on which keys were struck. However, only certain chords could be obtained. This kind of clavichord was called a fretted clavichord, and by 1440 it had attained a full chromatic range of three octaves. Unfretted clavichords, which had one key to each string, did not appear until the eighteenth century. Their compass reached five octaves, although like all clavichords they were very quiet.

The clavichord has one unique characteristic among keyboard instruments. By moving the key slightly up and down after striking it, a *vibrato* can be obtained. Although its volume range is so limited, the use of vibrato can give great expression to clavichord music.

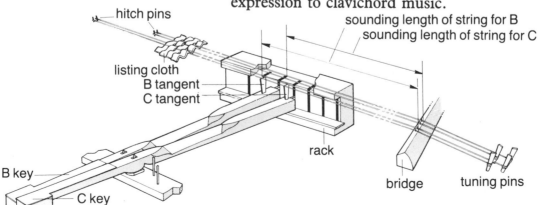

hitch pins

sounding length of string for B
sounding length of string for C

listing cloth
B tangent
C tangent

rack

bridge   tuning pins

B key

C key

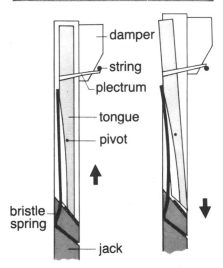

As the spinet jack goes up, the spring forces the quill against the string, so that it plucks the string. Coming down, the spring allows the centre of the jack to bend away, so that the quill does not pluck the string again, and the damper stops it sounding.

Above right: In the 'mother and child' double virginal, the small instrument above can be played on its own. It also sounds when the keys in the lower instrument are played, as the jacks from it operate the backs of the keys in the 'child'.

Right: Octave spinet, made in Italy at the beginning of the 17th century

Spinet and Virginal

Methods of using a keyboard to pluck a set of taut strings developed in the fifteenth century. At its far end, each key had a wooden jack containing a quill or leather *plectrum*. As the key was pressed, the jack rose and the quill or tongue plucked the string. When the key was released, the jack fell back but the quill or tongue pivoted away from the string so that it did not pluck it again. At the same time, a *damper* on the jack stopped the string sounding.

Large instruments using this method are known as harpsichords, while smaller instruments are called spinets and virginals. Spinets have wedge-shaped cases with the strings lying at an angle diagonal to the keyboard. A virginal has a rectangular case with the strings running from left to right, at right angles to the keys. Spinets and virginals became popular during the sixteenth century as instruments in the home. Some virginals had two keyboards side by side so that duets could be played on them. Like the clavichord, the spinet and virginal remained in favour until the piano became popular in the late eighteenth century.

Harpsichord

Profile
First example: 1440
Made of: wooden case;
metal strings; ivory or
wooden keys
Compass: 5½ octaves
Length: 190–235 cm

The harpischord contains a jack mechanism similar to the spinet or virginal to pluck its strings. However, it is a much larger instrument, with a case nearer to the size of a grand piano and, like the piano, the strings run directly away from the keyboard, parallel to the keys themselves.

Most harpsichords have horizontal strings. The earliest survivor of this kind is an Italian instrument of 1521. It has one set of strings and one manual or keyboard. By the end of the century however, makers were beginning to develop the instrument and further sets of strings were added, together with one or even two more manuals.

At first the extra strings were tuned to a different pitch from the rest of the instrument, so that a player could perform a piece of music in a different key from that in which it was written, by simply moving to the extra manual.

By the mid-seventeenth century, the manuals were tuned to the same pitch, and stops were used to give different sounds. These are operated like organ stops, and can either couple together strings at different octaves, or vary the way the sound is made. The harp stop, for example, moves leather pads to mute the strings, while the lute stop shifts the quill to give a lighter tone. By setting different stops for the different manuals it is possible to produce contrasting sounds by changing manual during a piece of music.

This modern English harpsichord has three hand-operated stops just above the left-hand end of the keyboard.

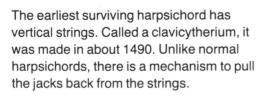

The earliest surviving harpsichord has vertical strings. Called a clavicytherium, it was made in about 1490. Unlike normal harpsichords, there is a mechanism to pull the jacks back from the strings.

The 20th-century revival of the harpsichord was largely due to the brilliant Polish harpsichordist Wanda Landowska, seen here at a two-manual instrument of her own design.

Domenico Scarlatti, painted in 1740, was a great 18th-century virtuoso.

The bright sound of the harpsichord and its variety of tone made it popular with composers and performers, who played it both as a solo instrument and while directing an orchestra from the keyboard. The harpsichord reached its peak early in the eighteenth century with the music of Domenico Scarlatti, who developed keyboard playing to new and brilliant heights in his 555 single-movement sonatas. During the same period J S Bach was also writing for the instrument, notably the *Goldberg Variations* and the *Italian Concerto*.

However, although the tone of the harpsichord could be varied with stops, the changes were abrupt and it was not possible to make the instrument get gradually louder or softer. In the late eighteenth century a pedal was added to raise and lower a lid or shutters over the strings in order to swell or diminish the sound, and another pedal could produce stop changes without the player's hands leaving the keyboard. But these improvements did not prevent the harpsichord from declining in popularity as the piano was developed.

By about 1800 nearly all new keyboard music was being written for the piano, and even music written for the harpsichord and the smaller string keyboard instruments was being played on the new instrument. It wasn't really until the twentieth century that the harpsichord began to be widely played again, for performing both earlier music and pieces written for it by contemporary composers.

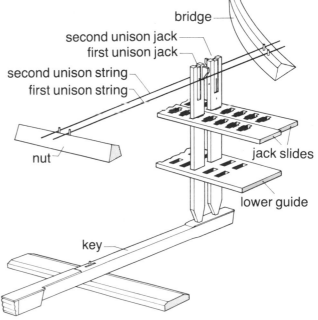

bridge

second unison jack
first unison jack

second unison string
first unison string

nut

jack slides

lower guide

key

In the harpsichord mechanism each key operates two jacks simultaneously, sounding two strings tuned to the same pitch.

The first pianos

The piano grew out of instrument makers' desire to create an instrument of equivalent size and power to the harpsichord with greater possibilities of *dynamic* control through the keys. The first attempts date from the fifteenth century when a keyed zither, called the 'dulce melos', was made in which metal hammers at the ends of keys struck strings.

Using hammers to strike the strings of a keyboard instrument was tried again by the Italian instrument maker, Bartolomeo Cristofori, at the very end of the seventeenth century. The pressure of the fingers on the keys could be varied to make the music soft (*piano*) or loud (*forte*), and the new instrument became known as the pianoforte.

These days early instruments are often called fortepianos to distinguish them from modern pianos.

Cristofori pioneered most of the features of the modern piano. These include the escapement, an arrangement of levers that sets the hammer moving as the key is pressed but allows it to fall back from the string after striking it. The levers also raise a damper from the string, so that it continues to sound until the key is released. Cristofori's pianos had two strings for each note, and he also invented the *una corda* (one string), a hand-operated lever that shifted the keys so that only one string sounded, giving a softer tone. This principle survives in the soft pedal of today's grand pianos.

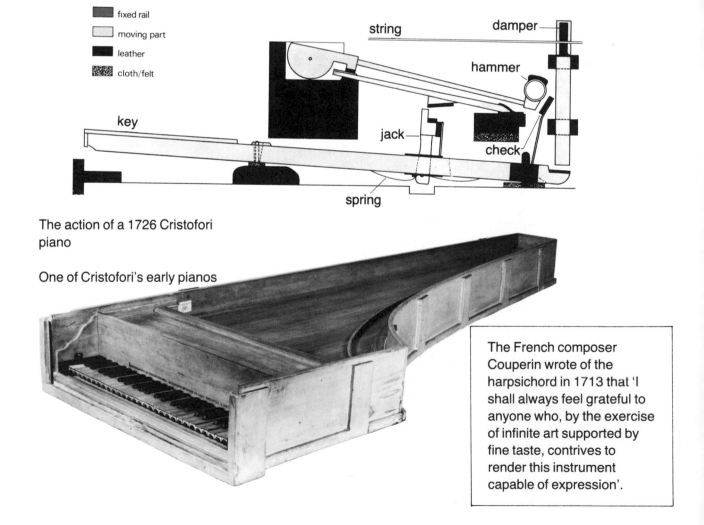

fixed rail
moving part
leather
cloth/felt

string

damper

hammer

key

jack

check

spring

The action of a 1726 Cristofori piano

One of Cristofori's early pianos

The French composer Couperin wrote of the harpsichord in 1713 that 'I shall always feel grateful to anyone who, by the exercise of infinite art supported by fine taste, contrives to render this instrument capable of expression'.

The orphica was a small portable piano, as shown above, made in the late 18th and early 19th centuries, which could be played on the lap. The singer Michael Kelly wrote: 'I had pen, ink, music paper and a small pianoforte put upon the table with our wine'.

In mid-eighteenth century Germany, Johann Stein improved the action of the instrument to produce a lighter touch and more even tone. His pianos delighted Mozart, enabling the composer to produce delicate but expressive piano music. Early pianos resembled harpsichords in shape, but from 1740 square pianos were made in the shape of clavichords or virginals. These were small and inexpensive, and became particularly popular in England, where J C Bach gave the first public piano recital on a square piano in 1768.

From the 1780s the grand piano developed in Britain with the work of John Broadwood. His instrument had two pedals as in modern pianos. One was a soft pedal and the other a pedal that sustained the sound after the key was released by raising all the dampers from the strings. Broadwood also strengthened the frame to allow greater tensioning of the strings, thus producing a more powerful sound, and he extended the range to six octaves. Such an instrument enabled Beethoven to compose piano music of unprecedented power and dramatic expression.

A mid-19th century Swiss family concert, in which the square piano can easily be seen on the right, the keyboard cover folded open to form a music stand

Modern grand piano

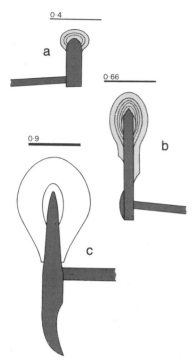

Three sets of string and hammer – all sounding the same note – showing how they became thicker and larger as the instrument was developed: a) Heilmann c1785; b) Broadwood c1823; c) Steinway c1970

The music of Mozart and Beethoven played on a square or fortepiano sounds quite different from the same music played on a modern grand piano. The hammers of older pianos were covered with leather, giving a harder tone than today's felt-tipped hammers. The overall sound is lighter and less rich.

In the 1820s and 1830s, the grand piano underwent several basic developments. First was the double escapement action, which keeps the hammer poised near the string when the key is still held down. This allows faster repeated notes and trills. Then came the introduction of felt for the hammers, which enabled heavier hammers to be used. Frames made entirely of iron were adopted, so that the strings could be stretched to greater tensions to gain more brilliance of tone. Finally, overstringing or cross-stringing was introduced in which the bass (low) strings are positioned at an angle across the tenor (middle) strings. This makes the piano more compact and balances the tension on the frame (which may reach as much as thirty tonnes overall), and the bass and tenor strings reinforce each other, producing a richer tone.

Pianos now have three different arrangements of strings: a single string for each note in the bass, double strings in the tenor range and triple strings for the treble. The range is usually a minimum of seven octaves from A to A, though often pianos have an extra three treble keys extending to C. Many modern grand pianos have a third central pedal that sustains notes sounding when the pedal is pressed but not those played after. This means that a chord can be sustained as detached, staccato notes are played with two hands.

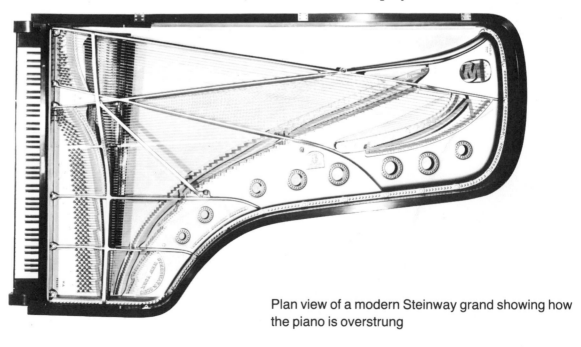

Plan view of a modern Steinway grand showing how the piano is overstrung

Upright piano

Jazzman Thelonious Monk playing an upright piano in a New York club, with Charles Mingus (bass) and Roy Haynes (drums). The microphone is amplifying the piano.

A modern concert grand piano is some three metres long: much too large for the average home. Although smaller grand pianos exist, many homes have upright pianos that take up less space.

Although small square pianos were built for use in the home in the eighteenth century, the upright piano did not develop from them. The early instruments had the strings parallel to the keyboard, restricting their range. An upright piano has the strings at a right-angle to the keyboard.

Early upright designs looked like grand pianos turned on their end. The strings did not extend far below the keyboard and towered above the player. The modern upright, in which the strings extend to the foot of the case, dates from 1800 and was invented independently in Austria and the United States. A new action had to be developed to allow the hammers and dampers to strike and mute vertical strings.

Upright pianos also have iron frames and are overstrung to get a rich sound. The main difference between an upright and a grand piano is in the bass. The bass strings of an upright are generally shorter and thicker, producing a less full tone. And because the strings cannot be uncovered as in the grand piano with the lid up, the overall sound may be not quite so powerful and brilliant.

The upright piano became very popular as a domestic instrument in the nineteenth and early twentieth centuries. More recently, new man-made materials have been used in the piano action, to make it lighter and more accurate, as builders have tried to make smaller instruments without losing tone quality.

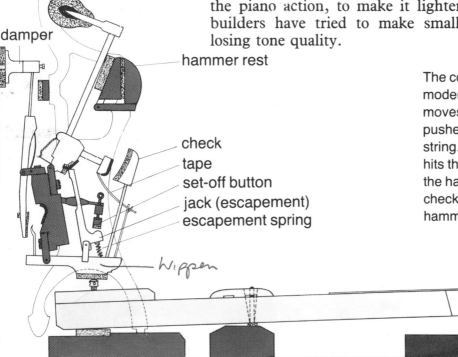

damper

hammer rest

check
tape
set-off button
jack (escapement)
escapement spring

wippen

The complicated action of a modern upright piano: the key moves the jack which rises and pushes the hammer on to the string. As the jack goes back it hits the set-off screw and it and the hammer fall back to the check. A swift return of the hammer is helped by the tape.

Piano music

The development of the piano has had a great effect on music over the past two centuries and the piano sonatas and concertos of Mozart and Beethoven are masterly works that were the result of fundamental piano developments between about 1760 and 1820. With the perfection of the grand piano by the mid nineteenth century, brilliant performers such as Chopin and Liszt were able to exploit the instrument's new capabilities, producing music that was romantic and flamboyant.

At the end of the nineteenth century, Debussy discovered a new range of sounds in the piano, obtaining beautiful effects with the pedals and creating an entirely new kind of impressionist music. Ravel continued this style, adding the bravura of Liszt. Bartók on the other hand exploited the percussive qualities of the piano. Writing in the first half of this century, both he and Stravinsky used the piano as an orchestral instrument, making it an extension of the percussion section.

Since the 1940s, composers such as Boulez, Stockhausen and Cage have written piano music which exploits the instrument's potential to the full. Experimenting with its extreme possibilities they contrast not only the highest and lowest pitches, but also the loudest and quietest sounds that the instrument will make. John Cage in particular has experimented with what he called 'prepared piano'. Various objects from bolts and screws to dampening materials such as erasers are placed in the instrument before it is played, usually according to careful instructions from the composer. By interfering with the mechanism, and particularly the strings, a whole new range of sounds is produced which can be altered for each piece or even for each performance.

A piano as part of the orchestra in Messiaen's *Turangalîla Symphony*

A typical prepared piano with screws and other objects placed inside

Pianists

The Italian, Pollini, playing a concerto for piano with orchestra

Below: A solo recital by Daniel Barenboim, also famous for concerto playing and conducting

Alicia de Larrocha, the Spanish pianist famous for her interpretations of the music of her country

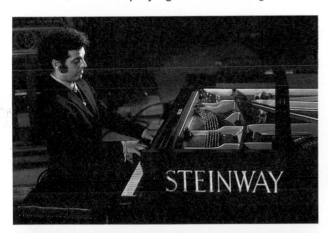

One of the great pianists of the century, Vladimir Horowitz, in a solo recital

Left: Jazz pianist Oscar Peterson who applies a classical technique to his jazz playing

Keyboard chimes

The Russian composer Tchaikovsky, who first heard the celeste on a trip to Paris, and was so impressed by its tone that he included it in his ballet *The Nutcracker*

Below: An orchestral celeste

Two further keyboard instruments exist that do not belong to either the wind or string keyboard families. They both use a keyboard to make bell-like sounds, but there the resemblance between them ends, for one is as small and quiet as the other is huge and sonorous. These instruments are called the celeste and carillon.

Celeste

The celeste (also called the celesta) looks like a small upright piano. It is played with a standard keyboard and has a range of four octaves extending upwards from middle C. The keys are connected via a piano action to hammers that strike metal bars hanging inside the case. The bars are suspended over wooden boxes that resonate to give a soft and delicate chiming sound.

The celeste is played in orchestras, generally to produce decorative effects. It was invented by August Mustel in 1886 and its sound fascinated Tchaikovsky, who used it to represent the Sugar Plum Fairy in his ballet *The Nutcracker*. The celeste is also featured prominently in *Music for Strings, Percussion and Celeste* by Bartók.

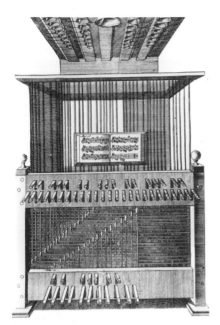

Carillon baton keyboard showing position of bells above

Carillon

A carillon is a set of bells that are tuned to the notes of the chromatic scale so that they can play melodies. A modern carillon has a range of up to six octaves, and the lowest bells may weigh as much as eighteen tonnes. The bells are mounted in a tower and the clappers are linked to a keyboard and pedalboard for the lowest notes. A piano keyboard cannot produce enough force to make the bells sound, so the carillon has a baton keyboard. Usually, this consists of rounded oak sticks, about 2 cm in diameter. Those in the upper row (the 'black notes' of the piano) are 9 cm long, those in the lower ('white notes') row are 16 cm long.

The batons are struck by the player's closed hands, usually with leather gloves protecting the fingers. Rollers and wires transmit the movements on the keyboard to the clappers of the bells, and even though various counter-weights are used to make the action as light as possible, the player needs to be physically srong to get an even sound from the bells.

There is a school of carillonists at Mechlin, and most players make this instrument their life's work, writing their own arrangements and adapting to instruments of different size, since modern carillons can have as few as twenty-five bells, or as many as forty-nine. The playing technique produces fairly simple music without thick chords, and more complex pieces can be performed with automatic mechanisms. Carillons evolved in Belgium and surrounding countries in the sixteenth and early seventeenth centuries. They died out in the nineteenth century but have been revived in this century.

In Britain, most bell towers are designed for change ringing with a team of players, each of whom pulls a rope directly connected to one of a set of bells. Music is made by varying the sequence in which the ropes are pulled. Change ringing has a long tradition attached to it, and some of the more famous sequences have names such as Grandsire Triples, which refers to the grouping of the changes in threes. A British bell tower tends to have fewer bells than the number needed for even the smallest carillon, and they have never achieved the popularity they have in the USA, Holland and Belgium, for this reason.

A carillon baton keyboard being played

> The largest carillon in the world is the Laura Spelman Rockefeller Memorial Carillon at Riverside Church in New York City, United States. It contains 74 bells weighing a total of over 100 tonnes. Its lowest bell is the largest tuned bell in the world and measures more than 3 metres across.

Keyboard terms

bore: interior of an organ pipe, the shape of which affects the tone quality

chromatic keyboard: one containing all twelve notes of the octave, a semitone apart

damper: felt or leather pad which, when pressed against string, stops the vibrations

dynamic: degree of loudness or softness

feet: one foot is equivalent to 30.5 centimetres

great: larger or main manual of a two-manual organ

hammer: the part of the mechanism of a piano or celeste which hits the string or bar. Usually wooden, covered with padding

jack: the part of the mechanism of a plucked-string keyboard instrument which contains the sprung *quill* and moves past the string

lip: edge of hole in pipe against which the air is split to produce vibrations

pallet: valve

plectrum: plucking device used also by string players such as guitarists and lutenists

positive: smaller manual of a two-manual organ. Also a single-manual portable organ

quill: plucking device mounted on a *jack* made either from leather or the lower part of a bird's feather

rollerboard: the part of the linking mechanism of *trackers* from an organ keyboard to its pipes in which vertical movement of keys is conveyed sideways, allowing a key to operate a pipe not directly above it

stop: a knob or button used to control sets of pipes in an organ. Each stop controls part of

the tone quality of the instrument, and stops are used singly or together

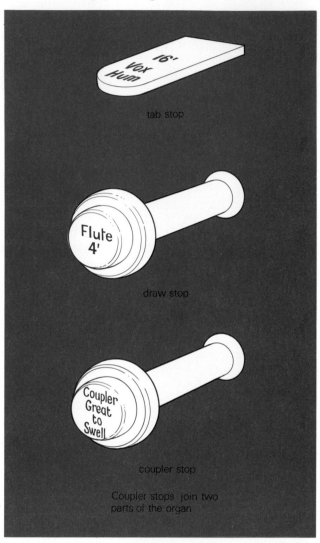

tab stop

draw stop

coupler stop

Coupler stops join two parts of the organ

tangent: the part of the mechanism of a clavichord which strikes the string. Made of brass

tracker: a strip of material, usually wood, connecting a key with its *pallet* or valve, or with the *rollerboard* of an organ

unison: notes identical in pitch

vibrato: a rapidly repeated variation of pitch, so slight that the note is considered to remain the same

Voice

Some different kinds of singer

The voice was the very first musical instrument, and it is the only one that is actually part of the performer.

The singer has a lot of advantages. There is no need to cart an instrument around like a double bass player, no need to be prepared to play a different instrument in every concert hall like a pianist, and no need to tune the voice, polish it, oil it or rosin it.

Yet because it *is* part of the singer it is instantly affected by a cold, a cough, or too many late nights. When a singer warms up before a concert, or uses a throat spray, it's because, as the most intimate musical instrument of all, the voice is also the most sensitive and needs most care and attention.

1 choristers, who often start their training at the age of six or seven
2 a group of gospel singers
3 folk singers, singing traditional songs

What makes the sound?

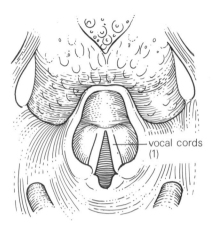

The larynx, viewed through
a laryngoscope

Like all other noises, the sound of the voice is made by the vibration of air.

The part played by a string, reed or lips in the case of an instrument, is taken by the vocal cords (1) in the case of the voice. These two hard membranes are about 15 mm in length in an adult male, about 11 mm in length in the female. They stretch from front to back of the *larynx* or *voice box* (2) – the valve guarding the entrance to the *trachea* or *windpipe* (3). You can easily find the voice box: it is the protruberance known as the *Adam's apple.*

Air sent at speed up the windpipe from the *lungs* (following their contraction as a result of the *diaphragm* (4) being raised and contracted) blows the vocal cords apart. There is then a fall in pressure in the windpipe so the cords touch each other again. The process is repeated, very quickly, and the rhythmic vibrations of the cords produce sound.

The human voice can produce an amazing range of different types of sounds. A North African singer prefers a sound very different from a singer in the Hebrides; a French church choir sounds very different from one in England.

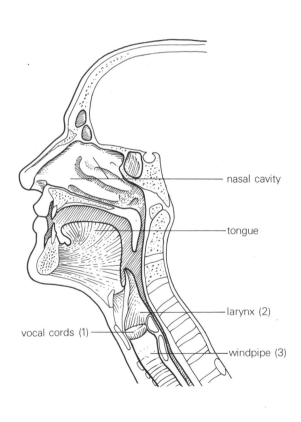

Detail of the head and neck

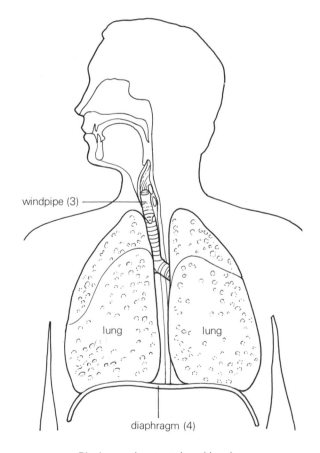

Diaphragm, lungs, neck and head

How does the singer make different notes?

The quality of the voice depends to some extent on the size and shape of the various cavities. You will notice, for example, that many outstanding singers have large mouths. It was jokingly said that the famous tenor Caruso was capable of holding a complete egg in his mouth. The vowel sounds being sung also affect the vocal quality.

Two very different kinds of singing: a Sudanese accompanying herself on a drum (far right), and a Yugoslavian using a gusle to accompany his song (right)

As well as housing the vocal cords, the larynx contains a number of muscles which can move the cords on each other (shown by the arrows). As in the case of strings and air columns, lips and reeds, the shorter or tighter the vibrating cords the higher the note, the longer or more relaxed the lower the note.

Higher air pressure causes faster vibrations, and vice versa. Try singing a very low note and then a very high note. Which needs most effort?

The singer hears in his or her mind the note about to be sung, adjusts the air pressure and the tension of the vocal cords by use of the appropriate muscles, breathes out – and produces the note.

Any voice, whether a high female voice or a deep male voice, has three main *registers*. The quality of the voice in each register is different as its tone depends to a great extent on the parts of the vocal cords vibrating.

The term *head voice* is used for the higher notes, *middle voice* for the medium range and *chest register* for the lower notes. But these are not really accurate descriptions as all sounds made by the vocal cords are amplified by resonance in the chest, mouth and head cavities.

In the less often used *falsetto register* the cords are brought together and only a short length vibrates. This produces notes of a very high pitch.

The voice of a boy is said to *break* when the vocal cords reach a length which causes the voice to drop in pitch.

Male voices

James Bowman

Placido Domingo

Counter-tenor

The counter-tenor is an unusually high male voice. It is strong and incisive, clear and flexible. Used in the sixteenth century, it has only recently been revived in England by Alfred Deller, and composers are writing for it again.

Tenor

The tenor is the supreme male display voice. Physically delicate, it has to be treated with care. Often in opera it is the voice of the ardent lover, of the soulful poet. The *Helden-tenor* specialises in heroic parts, the *lyric tenor* is a lighter voice.

Geraint Evans

Boris Christoff

Baritone

Most men naturally sing notes in the baritone range. It is as powerful as the bass voice, yet without the heaviness, as flexible as the lower part of the tenor range with some of the clarity of the tenor's voice, but fuller.

Bass

The bass voice is the deepest of all. The true bass has a full, round quality with sufficient edge to give it focus. It is capable of both immense power and subtle suggestion. The *basso profundo* specialises in the lowest register of all.

Female voices

Soprano

The soprano is the highest female voice, and like the tenor, is often given 'display' parts. The very high *coloratura* part requires a soprano to sing immensely demanding and highly ornamented music. A boy's voice in the soprano range is called a treble.

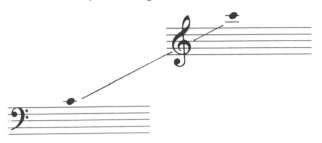

Leontyne Price

Mezzo-soprano

The mezzo-soprano uses the higher notes of the contralto and the lower notes of the soprano. She thus has an extremely wide and expressive range. Hers is a voice capable of expressing a variety of emotions and feelings.

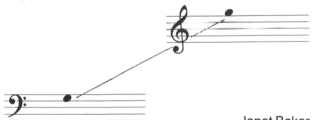

Janet Baker

Contralto

As the deepest female voice, the contralto has a full quality. Composers often use the lower contralto voice to contrast with the two higher ranges. The equivalent male voice (obtained by singing *falsetto*) is the alto.

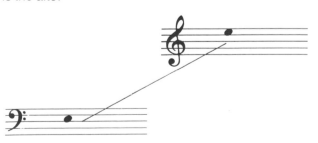

Carolyn Watkinson

How song began

By the 15th century, choirs were a regular feature of church music. This one is accompanying a mass.

Right: Church choirs have been a feature of English village life for several hundred years. It was a choir like this on which Thomas Hardy based his novel *Under the Greenwood Tree*.

Pope Gregory, who lived in the 6th century, dictating Gregorian chant to a scribe

Trying to discover how song began is much more difficult than learning about early instruments. These can last for centuries, and players are often shown in ancient sculptures and paintings. But to draw a voice is impossible.

Some information about early singing exists in the writings of the Ancient Greeks, which describe the way in which epic tales – long poems telling stories of heroic deeds – were sung by bards, often to a large gathering of people. Simple choral songs are also described in Greek and Roman literature, and in the Old Testament of the Bible. These appear to have served particular functions: as work songs, victory songs, or lullabies, for example. The Ancient Greeks accompanied songs on the lyre, and included them in their plays.

Vocal music of the church

Singing plays an important part in religious worship in many parts of the world. The earliest Christian hymn to survive complete with melody dates from the third century, and of course hymns are still being written today.

In almost every religion *chanting* is found: a very restricted type of singing, using only a few notes.

Plainsong, a kind of chanted melody, was adopted by the Christian church very early in its history. Gregorian chant (so called because St Gregory both supervised the Roman choir school and edited the collection of chants) was initially developed in the eighth century but was added to over the following 400 years. Much of it is still used in the mass today.

How song developed

A troubadour. These poet-musicians wrote in the Provençal dialect, whilst trouvères wrote in French.

Although there are descriptions of non-religious songs in the literature of the tenth and eleventh centuries, very few of the songs have survived as written music, so we don't know exactly what they sounded like.

From the twelfth century onwards, however, there are several examples of the songs sung by the *troubadours* and *trouvères* of France.

These were poet-musicians, many of them of high social status, who sang to mainly aristocratic audiences about love. Troubadours lived and worked in southern France, in Provence, and trouveres in northern France. Since French was the accepted language of poetry in England as well, some of them also sang in English courts.

Jongleurs were singers, players and acrobats who travelled around Europe also during the middle ages. Not much is known about them but they probably performed to the general public, not just aristocrats.

Bottom left: Part of a trouvère song, written in the late 13th century. The illuminated letter at the top shows the author Adam the Hunchback.

Below: In 14th-century Europe, groups of minstrels or jongleurs would arrive at a town in a procession like this, painted about 1380.

Singing in parts

If two people sing the same tune at the same time, one beginning five notes above the other, this gives some idea of the likely sound of the earliest *polyphony*: singing in parts. Singing at a fixed interval in this way was called organum, but by the year 1000 the voices were already much freer in their movement. Two hundred years later, the monks of Reading Abbey were singing *Sumer is icumen in.*

Sumer is icumen in

On the left is the manuscript dating from 1250 of this *rota* or round-song. A modern translation of the words and music is on the right. At the bottom is a part for tenor and bass consisting of repeated notes, called a 'pes', whilst the rest of the tune can be sung as a round, each new voice starting when the previous voice gets to the cross in the first line. The Latin instructions are also translated here: 'This round can be sung by four fellows, but must not be performed by fewer than three, or at least two, apart from those who have the *pes*, and when he shall have come to the first note after the cross, another begins, and so on with the rest. But each shall pause at the written rests, and not elsewhere, for the duration of one long note. One singer repeats this (the first *pes*) as often as necessary, observing the rest at the end. Another sings this (the second *pes*) with a rest in the middle but not at the end, at which point he at once repeats the beginning.'

Sum-mer is a com-ing in,— loud-ly sing cuck-oo;

Groweth seed and bloweth mead and springeth wood a-new:

Sing cuck - oo. Ewe bleat-eth af-ter lamb, loweth

af-ter calf the cow, Bul-lock starteth, buck reverteth

Mer-ry sing cuck-oo Cuck-oo, cuck-oo,—

will singest thou cuck-oo Nor cease thou nev-er now

These two bar parts sing continuously

Sing cu - cu nu, sing cu - cu

Sing cu - cu Sing cu-cu nu.—

Solo song

The motet

Motets were written between the thirteenth and eighteenth centuries and were compositions for several voices. They were *polyphonic* in style, each voice moving independently, but with all the parts fitting together. Although they were usually without instrumental accompaniment, this varied over the centuries. Often they were on sacred themes with Latin texts, but at times non-religious texts were used.

The madrigal

The term madrigal was used in sixteenth-century Italy to describe non-religious songs for several singers. Poems of all kinds were used, including those on themes such as love and nature. Madrigals were sung both for private entertainment, by groups of amateur musicians, and in public, as part of dramatic performances involving costumes and scenery. Although it originated in Italy, the madrigal was also developed by the English composers, Morley, Weelkes and Wilbye.

Away from the church, folk song also flourished. Often it told a story through a number of verses, each sung to the same melody.

Composers of the eighteenth century such as Haydn, used this simple folk-song treatment in their compositions for voice with keyboard accompaniment. Franz Schubert, at the beginning of the nineteenth century, realised that the accompaniment could help the singer to express the meaning of the song. His piano parts were often written as a 'musical picture', varying slightly in each verse so as to give more dramatic effect to the words.

Schumann, Brahms and Wolf further developed these techniques. Their songs, all with German words, are the speciality of the lieder singer (*Lied* is the German for 'song').

In this century, the composers Mahler and Strauss used an orchestra to accompany the lieder singer. Strauss set contemporary poetry, while Mahler also set folk songs and translations of Chinese poetry.

A 16th-century painting of four madrigal singers. The man seems to be beating time with his hand.

The composer Franz Schubert playing the piano, with his friend, the singer Johann Vogl, on his right

Anatomy of oratorio

Oratorio came into existence during the mid seventeenth century, in Italy. Handel, Bach, Haydn, Mendelssohn and more recently Elgar and Walton all wrote oratorios. Involving soloists, choir and orchestra, they tell a story without action, costumes or scenery.

On Good Friday 1729 J S Bach's *St Matthew Passion* had its first performance. It is one of the greatest musical works ever composed.

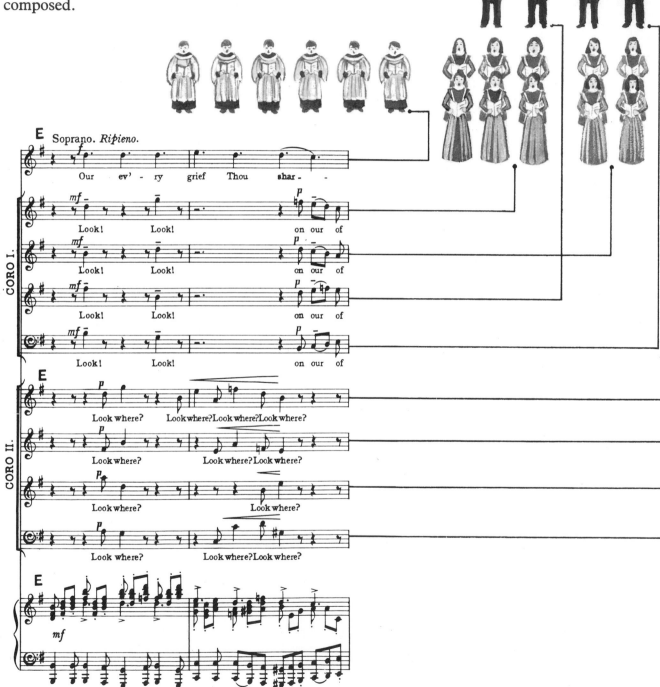

There are four principal soloists, two choirs (each with an orchestra), and a treble choir, together with a small group of soloists usually drawn from one of the two main choirs. At times the congregation joins in the singing of chorales: hymns of the Lutheran church.

Oratorio incorporates a style of singing called *recitativo*, in which a solo voice is accompanied by a single instrument (often a harpsichord or organ) which often plays a series of chords. Whilst simple storytelling is usually sung in a *recitativo* style, the soloists also have extended *arias* which concentrate on one aspect of the story and are more song-like.

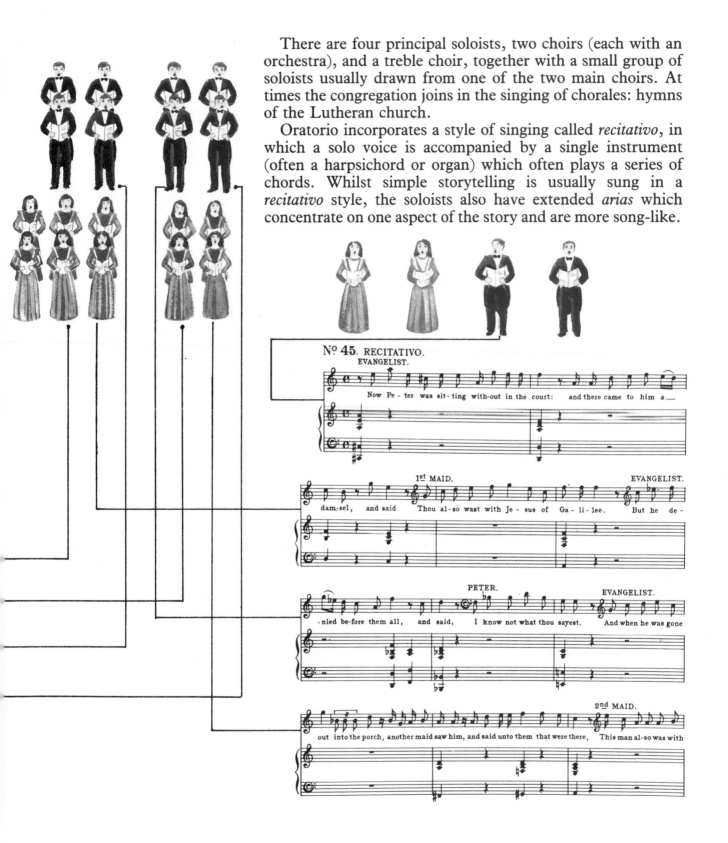

Nº **45**. RECITATIVO.
EVANGELIST.

Now Peter was sitting without in the court: and there came to him a—

1st MAID.   EVANGELIST.

damsel, and said Thou also wast with Jesus of Galilee. But he de-

PETER.   EVANGELIST.

-nied before them all, and said, I know not what thou sayest. And when he was gone

2nd MAID.

out into the porch, another maid saw him, and said unto them that were there, This man also was with

The birth of opera

The first operas – music dramas – were written and performed during the last years of the sixteenth century in Italy, and were part of a developing interest in combining music for the voice with dramatic action.

Spectacles involving instrumentalists, costumed singers, actors and lavish scenery had been performed at the courts of the Italian nobility for the previous hundred years. Sometimes these were designed for the breaks between the acts of a play, but the most lavish were performed on special occasions such as christenings and weddings. Another form of entertainment was the pastoral play – set in the country – which involved singing and instrumental music.

Early operas incorporated aspects of these usually rather brief dramatic and musical events, using more highly developed musical forms and often more complicated stories. There was a great deal of interest in Ancient Greek myth at the time, and these were used as the subjects of the operas.

The greatest of the early opera composers was Claudio Monteverdi (c1567–1643). From his first opera, *Orfeo* (1607), to his last, *The Coronation of Poppea* in 1642, he developed the operatic form, bringing together an expressive *recitativo* style which closely followed the phrase structure of the narrative, and arias and duets increasingly varied in their rhythm and melody.

Opera caught on quickly (the first public opera house was opened in Venice in 1637) and productions rapidly became increasingly spectacular. Ingenious machines enabled gods to descend from the clouds, and towns to be destroyed by earthquakes.

During the seventeenth and early eighteenth centuries staging became more and more complex, and acting increasingly formal. However, by the nineteenth century, the opportunities for vocal display offered by the aria led to the voice, and therefore the singer, becoming the most important part of opera.

The stage design for a scene in a series of music dramas, performed in Florence in 1589 to celebrate the wedding of Ferdinando de' Medici and Christine of Lorraine

The final scene from a recent English National Opera production of Monteverdi's *Coronation of Poppea*, showing the two principals in the story, Nero and Poppea

A scene from a recent production of Mozart's *The Magic Flute*. The sets were designed by the painter David Hockney.

The courtroom scene from John Gay's *The Beggar's Opera*. This engraving is taken from a painting by William Hogarth.

Opera outside Italy

During the seventeenth century France developed its own type of opera. Lully (1632–1687) was its first composer, followed by Rameau (1683–1764). French opera was formal and artificial, and usually had a group of singers called the chorus, and a ballet in each performance. (Even when Wagner's *Tannhäuser* was performed in Paris in 1861 he had to include a ballet.)

No other part of Europe during the eighteenth century had its own fully-developed style of opera. Instead they imported opera from Italy, performed in Italian often by Italian singers.

Opera buffa

Opera buffa began in Naples early in eighteenth century, and immediately became very popular. All kinds of subjects were set to music – romances, escape dramas – but they tended to be treated in a light-hearted way, with tuneful melodies. By the middle of the century the style had spread to Germany, where Mozart wrote the finest *opera buffa*, among them *Don Giovanni* and *The Marriage of Figaro*.

Opéra comique and Singspiel

Light-hearted plays, which included songs, were also established as a standard form in France by the middle of the eighteenth century, and were called *opéra comique*. Some of them actually made fun of the more stilted operas of Lully, and others made critical comments about political figures of the time. They were performed at court, in the theatres and in fairgrounds, but for several years at the beginning of the eighteenth century only licensed companies were allowed to perform. The poorer companies who did not have licences got round the law and performed as a dumbshow, with the actors miming their parts, placards displaying the words, and the audience encouraged to sing the songs.

Similar productions involving music linked by words became popular in England, with John Gay's *Beggar's Opera* in 1728, and the development of the German *Singspiel* towards the end of the eighteenth century. Some of the most popular operas ever written – Mozart's *Il Seraglio* and *The Magic Flute*, Weber's *Der Freischütz*, and Beethoven's *Fidelio*, for example – combine speech and song in this way.

Nineteenth-century opera

Above: Josef Hoffmann's stage design for the first production of Wagner's *Ring*
Below: In production, trolleys were used to push the rhinemaidens (supposedly swimming) around the stage.

Germany

One of the characteristics of German opera in the nineteenth century was the attempt by composers to establish a new art form in which all the different aspects of opera – words, music, and dramatic action – were carefully integrated.

Richard Wagner (1813–1883) dedicated his life to the project, and succeeded in the 'Ring' cycle of operas, eventually performed in a specially-designed opera house in Bayreuth, where there is still an annual Wagner festival.

The four operas making the 'Ring' are *Rhinegold*, *The Valkyrie*, *Siegfried* and *The Twilight of the Gods*. Each one is immensely long and they require a great deal of stamina from the lead singers. Unlike any other kind of opera, in which new melodies are used throughout and are not repeated, these four operas are organised on the principal of the *leitmotif*. Different tunes or chord sequences are introduced to represent each of the characters and important objects such as the Rhine, and these tend to return whenever the character or object is on stage or referred to. This new way of structuring the music helped Wagner to achieve his union of words, music and action.

Italy

Italian grand opera reached a peak in the works of Giuseppe Verdi (born like Wagner in 1813, died in 1901). *Aida*, *La Traviata*, *Rigoletto*, *Il Trovatore* and *Falstaff* (written when he was eighty) are performed and enjoyed in opera houses all over the world. During Verdi's lifetime his operas were extremely popular and they have remained so since. Certain songs have been used as symbols of Italian patriotism.

Operetta

The jester Jack Point is the central character in Gilbert and Sullivan's *Yeoman of the Guard.*

A scene from the film version of *My Fair Lady* in which Eliza Doolittle is taken to the races

In the 1850s in France, operetta, a style of comic or light opera, began to develop from *opéra comique*, absorbing some of the style of the vaudeville (a collection of unrelated songs). Offenbach was the first major composer in this style, with light, two-act operettas like *Pepito* and *Orpheus in the Underworld.*

Offenbach's work became popular in Vienna, where local composers Suppé and Zajc imitated the style. But soon the Viennese operetta took on a life of its own, with the work of Johann Strauss. He included exotic settings and dances (especially the Viennese waltz) in his work, in particular *Die Fledermaus* (1874). The next ten years were the golden age of Viennese operetta.

In England Offenbach's work influenced Arthur Sullivan who collaborated with playwright W S Gilbert to produce a particularly British style of clever and witty operetta. These works were known as the Savoy Operas, as they were performed at London's Savoy theatre.

In common with Parisian and Viennese operettas Gilbert and Sullivan's work found its way to the USA, and by the end of the last century operetta was a popular American form, with compositions by two European composers: Friml, who wrote *Rose Marie*, and Romberg, who wrote *The Student Prince* and *Desert Song.*

A moment in *Die Fledermaus* by Johann Strauss

Musical

The American musical theatre grew from European operetta, and flourished in the works of Jerome Kern. His show *Showboat* was one of the first of the musicals where every song added to character or plot. The work of Gershwin and Cole Porter (*Kiss Me Kate!*) led to musicals on a grander scale, with the tremendously successful partnerships of Rodgers and Hammerstein (*Oklahoma!* and *South Pacific*) and Lerner and Loewe (*My Fair Lady*).

Anatomy of a musical

Many musicals begin by being written for the theatre, and are then turned into recordings and films. One of the most famous is *West Side Story* which began as an idea of choreographer Jerome Robbins. He had already worked with composer Leonard Bernstein, on a ballet, and with author Arthur Laurents and lyricist Stephen Sondheim, they spent nine years working on the new musical. It was first produced in New York in 1957, and the stage version was later seen in all the major cities of the world. The original cast recorded the music, which was issued on disc and tape. In 1961 it was made into a film, and revived in New York in 1981.

Stage production
The basis of *West Side Story* was Shakespeare's *Romeo and Juliet*. The complicated plot revolves around the love of Tony and Maria, members of opposing gangs, the American Jets and Puerto Rican Sharks. The stage show involves a large cast, representing the gangs, and the orchestra and conductor in the pit below and in front of the stage.

The soundtrack musical recording is played back, as actress Natalie Wood (Maria) and actor Richard Beymer (Tony) are filmed, miming to the words.

Record production

The musical was separately recorded in a studio. Usually, for such a recording, the composer rearranges the tunes slightly so that instead of being part of the plot of the play, flowing into the action, they are self-contained. This often involves writing new beginnings and endings, so that the tunes are clearly separated on the record.

The recording is mixed into a final film soundtrack.

Filming

For a film of a musical, new music has to be written (the normal 'incidental' music of a film) and often the orchestrations and arrangements for the rest of the music are enlarged. Sometimes the original composer does this, but more often it is a studio musical director and a team of orchestrators. Often, too, the actors and actresses who play the main parts have the voices of professional singers recorded in their place on the soundtrack of the film. So the whole soundtrack is recorded again, with a studio orchestra and singers and, for *West Side Story*, Marni Nixon and Jimmy Bryant singing Maria and Tony.

Folksong

A modern English folksinger

The Hungarian composer Béla Bartók recording peasants singing. His own works were influenced by this folk music.

Right: Cecil Sharp, the English folksong collector, travelled to the Appalachian mountains in America to transcribe English songs which were still being sung there at the beginning of this century. Here he is transcribing a song with his assistant Maud Karpeles.

Folk music tends not to be written down but to be passed from musician to musician and held in people's memories. This is especially true of songs. Because there is no single written version, a song will change over the years with each new person who learns it. In Europe and America, because there is a strong tradition of written music, the distinction between folk music and other kinds of music is very strong. In other parts of the world, such as Africa, music is not usually divided in this way.

Today, by recording them, it is possible to preserve folksongs as they are performed. But before the days of recording, it was difficult to preserve traditional songs, as this had to be done by writing them down. Transcribing them was hard because the songs varied from person to person, and the rhythms and intonation were not easily written in conventional notation.

The English folksinger has a characteristic style without much variation in volume but with a lot of ornamentation: singing notes above and below those of the main tune to vary it or add emphasis to certain points in the music. Folksongs can be performed either unaccompanied or with a range of instruments. American folk music has many different styles because people from all over the world migrated to the USA, and kept their own musical traditions. The influence of British and other European music is mixed with that of Black Americans whose ancestors were brought over from Africa as slaves.

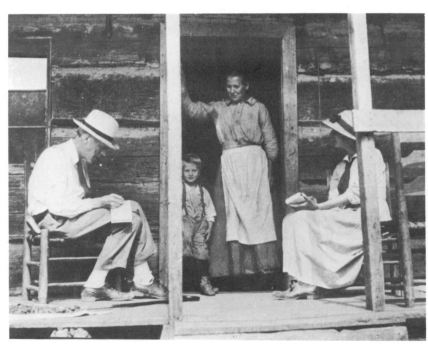

The harpist and singer Osian Ellis performing a song in the *penillion* style. An introduction is played on the harp before the song begins.

Improvised song

In many countries there is a type of song which is improvised by the singer – made up on the spot. In Wales the *penillion* is improvised to the accompaniment of the harp. The Portuguese *fado* often includes improvised sections. In the Middle East the *āvāz* is a style of singing used to recite poetry, and the *tahrir* involves complex *melisma* – the musical ornamentation of particular words of a song.

Work song

The shanty is a song designed to help sailors on sailing ships when working together as a team, by giving them a rhythm to keep to. Mainly sung in the nineteenth century, they can be divided into several categories depending on the particular task they were intended to provide the rhythm for: hauling the sails, heaving the anchor or pumping out the bilges.

Songs to help people work are sung all over the world, although these days they are often sung only for entertainment.

Most surviving worksongs, like shanties, relate to group activities, sometimes with a question and answer style. There are songs about railway construction and plantation work.

Below: Scottish women singing a waulking-song which has a rhythm suited to rubbing the feet over cloth to 'full' or finish it

Popular music

Country blues singer Mance Lipscomb

Bessie Smith, the 'Empress' of the blues, who recorded her blues singing with many jazz musicians, including duets with Louis Armstrong's trumpet

'Ma' Rainey's Band with Thomas Dorsey at the piano

Gospel

In the southern states of the USA, Black gospel music first began to be heard about 1900. Preachers often sang as part of their sermons, and the congregation joined in with hymn singing and off-beat clapping.

From about 1922, gospel choirs appeared on records, and songwriters such as Thomas Dorsey wrote a type of spiritual and choral song especially for these large groups. In the southern states today gospel choirs still flourish, and there are several festivals and competitions. There have been great solo gospel singers, in particular Mahalia Jackson, and Sister Rosetta Tharpe.

Blues

Another kind of singing, also developed by the Black people of the southern United States, is blues singing. The country or delta blues (named after the Mississippi delta) was a simple kind of folksong, with verses of two short lines which rhymed at the end. Sometimes the first line was repeated and followed with a third rhyming line. This was sung over a sequence of twelve bars of music which became the basis of rock and roll, and of much jazz music.

The people who sang the early country blues were seldom full-time singers. But there were some singers who joined the touring tent of vaudeville shows, who did make a living from singing, and these included 'Ma' Rainey, and the 'Empress of Blues', Bessie Smith. Both women sang a range of songs other than the eight- or twelve-bar blues, and they both made records later in their lives. 'Ma' Rainey had songs written for her by her pianist 'Georgia Tom', but he later turned to gospel writing under his real name Thomas Dorsey.

Muddy Waters and his band

Rhythm and Blues

As blues singers found their way northwards in the USA from the southern states, they settled in the big towns of the north. In particular, Chicago became the home to many blues singers and in its hard, urban environment, a new type of blues, with the singer accompanied by a 'rhythm section' of guitar, piano or organ, bass and drums, grew up. The singer and 'lead' guitar carried the tune (sometimes also with a saxophone or trumpet) and the rhythm emphasised the second and fourth beats of every bar, producing the famous 'blackbeat'.

'Muddy' Waters was a blues singer famous for this type of singing, having made his way north from the Mississippi Delta via Memphis.

Rock and Roll

In the 1950s, white musicians started to copy the work of the black rhythm and blues band, adding the 'hillbilly' songs of white American folk music to the twelve-bar blues. Many famous singers grew from this type of music, but the most famous was Elvis Presley.

Soul

In the 1960s, black gospel music and rhythm and blues came together in a style in which singers suggested strongly-felt emotions which included sighs, sobs and falsetto singing as part of the performance. The great exponents of soul are Ray Charles and Aretha Franklin.

The Kansas City blues shouters, most of whom worked with big bands, were a halfway stage between blues and R and B. Big Joe Turner (shown here), like Jimmy Rushing, sang with Count Basie's big band.

Elvis Presley at the height of his popularity, by which time he was famous for his sensational clothes and stage sets as well as for his music

In many forms of blues singing, the words carry major importance, and the tunes are repeated from verse to verse. But from the mid 1920s, when Louis Armstrong dropped the words of *Heebie Jeebies* during a record session, and went on to make up a nonsense vocal in a style called 'scat' singing, jazz singers improvised with the melody just as instrumentalists might, often taking similar liberties with words.

This has led to some outstanding jazz singing, where performers have developed techniques as impressive as classically-trained opera singers. Chief among such singers is Ella Fitzgerald, whose ordinary range covers almost all the contralto and soprano range, and with the use of falsetto, she can sing even higher. Another singer who has combined an equally impressive range with the harmonic and rhythmic complexity of modern jazz is Sarah Vaughan.

Jazz singing also developed with performers who were less concerned with range and flexibility than subtle changes of pitch and rhythm. Billie Holiday, who sang with every size of jazz accompaniment from big band to solo piano, was supreme in this art. Like most jazz singers she used a microphone to sing into, amplifying the sound of her voice.

Jazz singer Louis Armstrong (right) with crooner Bing Crosby (see facing page)

Billie Holiday singing in a crowded jazz club in the 1950s

The jazz singer Sarah Vaughan in action

Bob Dylan

Joni Mitchell, like Dylan, based her style on American folk music

Right: An early photograph of the Beatles. In the early 1960s their stage and recorded performances were sung over their electric guitar and drum accompaniment. As their music developed, and they worked increasingly on record, they used quite different accompaniments, from string quartets to brass bands, with elaborate tape editing of their songs.

The use of microphones and amplification led early on to developing special kinds of singing. Bing Crosby perfected the technique of 'crooning' (quiet sentimental singing) where amplification could project his quiet relaxed singing over a band or orchestra. He recorded from the mid 1920s until his death in 1977. He used the *head voice* in a much lower range than most classically-trained singers, and by slurring notes, or sometimes singing on consonants, he emphasised words in what was then a new and unusual way.

Crosby was one of a generation of American singers who found a huge public through radio, films and television. The new media of the twentieth century generated singer-entertainers, as well as adding new dimensions to the work of traditional concert and operatic singers.

The Beatles

Like Bing Crosby, the Beatles used the media to gain enormous international success. They combined much of the folk and music hall traditions of Britain with American Rock and Roll, to create a style which led pop music throughout the world for almost ten years from the mid 1960s. John Lennon and Paul McCartney wrote most of their songs, and they made many records and films. The Beatles were the most popular of a number of British groups at that time, including the Rolling Stones and The Who.

Bob Dylan

Just as the Beatles developed much of their music from Rock and Roll, Bob Dylan developed his style of folk and 'talking blues' singing from many types of American folk music. He demonstrated that pitch, phrasing and breath control were not the only elements of expressive singing. He has used a variety of accompaniments, from his own guitar and harmonica (or 'blues harp') playing, to full backing bands.

Rock singer Toyah in action

Bob Marley who was a leading reggae singer

Diana Ross, who, with the Supremes, was a leader of the Detroit MoTown style of soul singing

Frank Zappa, innovative singer and guitarist who sang with his band the Mothers of Invention

Electronic and mechanical

1 Fairground organ
2 Electric guitar
3 Synthesizer
4 Music computer

Here you can see a strange group of instruments in action: a fairground organ, an electric guitar, an electronic synthesizer and a music computer. Yet they all have something in common. They all need a source of power to make a sound.

Mechanical instruments

Most people like music, but not everyone plays an instrument or sings. Nowadays music can be heard on records or tape, but before recordings people used mechanical instruments to provide them with music.

Barrel organs

At the heart of the barrel organ is a set of pins fixed around a barrel. Each pin represents a note in the music. The barrel revolves, and the pins strike a set of levers. These move up and down, operating a mechanism that opens organ pipes so that air blows into the pipes and makes them sound.

The earliest known barrel organ was made by Arabs in the ninth century. It had only one pipe with a set of holes like a recorder. Flaps driven by a rotating pin barrel opened and closed the holes to produce the music. A water wheel turned the barrel, and cisterns filled with water to produce a supply of air to sound the pipe.

Later barrel organs had sets of pipes or reeds, and bellows to blow the air, and so could produce a wide and powerful range of sounds. Huge ones were built in the nineteenth century that sounded like military bands and orchestras. They were driven by clockwork, weights, steam or even electricity. In the early nineteenth century, barrel attachments were made for ordinary church organs, with a different barrel for each hymn tune. Street musicians wandered through cities entertaining people with barrel organs that they wound by hand.

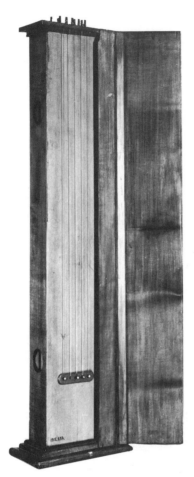

A copy of an Ancient Greek aeolian harp. It is hung up, and the wind sounds its strings.

The belfry at Bruges has one of the largest musical instruments in the world. It contains a carillon of 47 bells, dating back to 1528. Tunes are played on it by a pin-barrel mechanism and concerts are given throughout the year.

Right: A barrel organ, complete with monkeys, photographed in a London street at the beginning of this century

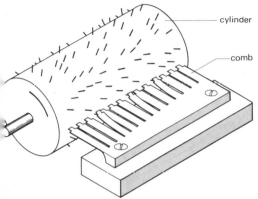

Above: Musical box mechanism

Right: A musical box inside a photograph album

Below: Both the pipe and tabor, and the flute are being played by mechanical figures, made by the Frenchman Jacques Vaucanson and shown to the public in London in 1742. The figures stopped the holes with automatic fingers and blew air into the mouthpieces. In the centre is a mechanical duck which quacked. Many types of singing birds were made, in all parts of Europe.

Musical boxes

The musical box works on the same principle as the barrel organ with the pins on a barrel plucking the teeth of a comb, graded in the length free to vibrate, to produce different pitches. This device was first used to sound the hour in clocks, and musical boxes did not become popular until about 1840. From about 1890 flat discs with pegs or projections began to replace pin barrels as the discs could be placed in the box as easily as changing a record. This kind of musical box became very popular for a while but was soon replaced by the gramophone or phonograph.

Musical dolls and monsters

The most amazing of all mechanical music makers were clockwork musical dolls and toys called automatons. Built in France and Switzerland in the eighteenth and nineteenth centuries, these mechanical marvels were taken by their makers on tour, and people flocked to see them.

Some other mechanical marvels of the early nineteenth century were designed to impress people by their size. The Panharmonicon, apparently named by the composer Haydn, was built in Austria by Joseph Gurk. It could produce 210 different sounds, all played mechanically. Another Panharmonicon, built by Joseph Maelzel, combined the sounds of over 300 instruments. It was worked by weights which drove cylinders with pins. Maelzel and Beethoven arranged Beethoven's 'Battle Symphony' for it, although the inventor later used Beethoven's orchestral version without his permission and incurred the composer's wrath.

The key-frame of a mechanical organ. The punched paper roll moves through a plate and the holes operate the notes.

A reproducing piano built by Steinway and Sons in 1904. The punched paper roll can be seen in the middle, above the keyboard.

Right: In this reproducing grand piano, built in 1926 by Erard-Ampico, the mechanism fits below the standard keyboard.

Air-driven instruments

Barrel organs and musical boxes could play pieces lasting only a few minutes and gave no expression to the music. These were replaced by new types of organ which were pneumatic (air-driven) and could play nonstop for hours if necessary. People could control them to produce their own interpretation of the music.

The notes of the music for these instruments are cut as holes or slots in a long paper roll or a folded length of cardboard. As the roll or card moves through the instrument, it passes over a plate with openings in it. The openings are connected to an air supply so that, as a hole or slot passes over one, air is puffed out or sucked in. This air movement causes an organ pipe to sound. These organs can still be heard at fairgrounds or rallies for old fairground machinery.

Player pianos

The new invention was soon applied to the piano, the most popular instrument in the home. Rolls were fitted into a piano with a pneumatic attachment, and the 'player' worked a pair of large pedals and hand controls to produce the music. The player piano or pianola, as it was called, became very popular from about 1900 onwards. The player could speed up or slow down the music and vary the phrasing and accents of the notes depending on the way he or she operated the instrument. Without any musical training, people could give good performances of their own. Those who already had a piano could buy an automatic playing attachment to fit over the keys.

Reproducing pianos

The most interesting mechanical instrument to us nowadays is a special kind of player piano called the reproducing piano. Famous musicians such as Debussy produced rolls that could be played on them. The piano was driven by electricity and reproduced the original performance very closely, including dynamics and expression. We can hear performances by composers and pianists who lived before good recording techniques developed.

However, as high-quality electrical recording developed in the 1930s, mechanical instruments finally died out. These days they are likely to be found and heard only in museums.

The keys on this reproducing piano are playing the opening chords of Grieg's Piano Concerto. The roll was made by Percy Grainger, and this performance was photographed after his death. The piano plays the solo part, to a speed set by the controls below the keyboard, and the orchestra plays the accompaniment.

Left: An American mechanical violin of 1907 consists of a real violin with a paper-roll pneumatic mechanism driving 'fingers' that stop the strings and turning discs that 'bow' them.

Electric instruments

Some musical instruments need electricity to make them sound. An electric guitar without the power switched on makes a note, but it is very soft, and the tone is very thin. Electricity is needed to amplify the sound that the guitar produces and, just as important, to give the sound a certain tone quality.

Getting a sound

An electric instrument, such as the electric guitar, needs to be connected to an amplifier and loudspeaker. Under the strings of the guitar is a pickup which changes the soft sounds made by the strings when they are plucked into very small electric signals. Every pitch gives a different signal which passes instantly along a wire or lead to the amplifier. Inside the amplifier, electricity is used to increase the strength of the signals before they travel to the loudspeaker, and come out as sound. The amplifier has volume and tone controls like those of a record player or radio, and often similar controls are placed on the guitar itself so that the player can make quick adjustments whilst playing.

The pickup

The pickup works like an electricity generator and consists of a coil of wire and a magnet. The strings on an electric guitar are made of metal and when plucked make the magnetic field around the coil vibrate, producing an electric signal.

Several other instruments have pickups, including the bass guitar. The electric piano has strings or thin metal rods, struck by hammers with a pickup under each of them.

Above: A Gibson electric guitar. The pickups are black and white panels with metal dots under the strings, and there are volume and tone controls.

Right: Blues player B B King with his Gibson guitar

Feedback can ruin a performance. If the volume is high the microphone picks up the sound coming from the speakers and amplifies it again, producing a loud whistling. To stop it, the microphone has to be covered and turned away from the speakers, and the volume turned down.

Using microphones

It is also possible to 'electrify' acoustic instruments. This can be done most simply by placing a microphone in front of the instrument which picks up the sound and changes it into electric signals in much the same way as a pickup does. Using a microphone makes the sound louder and with good quality equipment doesn't distort the tone of the instrument. In this way, it is possible to play an acoustic instrument amid loud electric instruments such as in a rock group.

Some musicians play acoustic instruments fitted with tiny microphones which allow them to move around while they are playing. Instruments that can be 'electrified' in this way include the violin, double bass, saxophone, trumpet and trombone.

Effects unit

Some rock guitarists play with their feet as well as their hands. On the floor are several pedal-operated 'effects units' that change the tone of the guitar sound. Any electric instrument can be treated in this way. Instead of going straight to the amplifier the sound from the instrument is passed through an effects unit first. This changes the signals produced by the pickup or microphone and alters the sound.

One of the most common effects is reverberation (reverb) or echo, which builds up the sound of the instrument. A wah-wah pedal makes the sound go 'wah' as it is pressed. A fuzz box produces a buzzy distorted sound, and other frequently-used effects are the phaser, flanger and chorus unit.

Left: An echo or reverb pedal, used by many rock bands. There are adjustable settings on the left. Echo and volume are controlled by the player's foot on the pedal.

Singer Randy Crawford holding a radio microphone

Vocals

Singers with electric bands need microphones so that their voices can be heard above the sound of the instruments. They have to be careful because if the microphone is held too close to the mouth the voice will be distorted.

Many singers use radio microphones which are not connected to the amplifier by wires, but have a small radio transmitter which produces signals that are picked up by a receiver on the amplifier. Sometimes these microphones are attached to singers or their clothing, leaving them much freer to move about. Singers in the musical theatre use microphones occasionally, as well as rock stars.

On stage

Above: Stuart Copeland with several microphones placed to pick up drums and cymbals

Below: Genesis in concert, with their sound equipment in the centre of the stage

The musicians in a rock band are only part of a large organization that puts such a show on the road. Out in the audience is the band's sound engineer, who is controlling the sound, and backstage is the road team, who transport tonnes of sound equipment and set it up in time for the concerts. Every band needs a certain amount of equipment to play on stage, and all bands have some basic equipment in common. Unlike classical orchestras, whose sound is affected by the acoustic of the hall in which they play, the music of a rock band is amplified and adjusted to fill any space, indoors or out.

Microphones and mixers

The members of the band have microphones or pickups on their instruments that produce electric signals. Electronic keyboard instruments produce signals directly when they are played and the drummer may have several microphones to pick up all the drums and cymbals. Leads from the instruments and microphones carry the signals to a mixer, which is set up in front of the band, usually among the audience. The mixer has a volume control for each signal entering it. The sound engineer sits at the mixer and controls the volume of each musician to make sure the music is balanced and that every member of the band can be heard properly. The mixer also has controls called equalizers which filter some sound frequencies, in order to give the best tone quality to each instrument or singer. The engineer may also add echo and move the sound between speakers.

Amplifier and Speakers

The mixer contains pre-amplifiers to amplify each of the input signals entering the mixer to a particular level. Then it mixes them together into one output signal, which goes to the main amplifier or power amplifier. This amplifier strengthens the signals so that they are powerful enough to work the loudspeakers. The speakers are usually placed at the sides of the stage. To spread the band out in stereo between the loudspeakers, the mixer produces two output signals and two power amplifiers are used – one for each speaker. In addition, small monitor speakers may be placed among the band so that the musicians can hear the whole band easily.

The Who between numbers in a concert, showing their on-stage amplification and speakers

Right: Sound engineer Geoff Hooper at his mixing desk during a Belgian festival. Each of the rows of controls operates one microphone input, and mixes them to one output signal.

Electric organs

Above: Close-up of a tone wheel showing the teeth

Below: Pianist Fats Waller, who recorded on the electric organ in the 1930s and 1940s

The electric organ is probably the most popular of all electric instruments. It can imitate the sounds of a huge pipe organ even though it is no larger than a small piano. And it can produce a wide range of other sounds as well. Most people play it as a solo instrument, though many rock bands include an electric organ.

How an electric organ works

Unlike other electric instruments, the electric organ does not make any sound at all, unless it is connected to a loudspeaker. Pressing the keys produces electric signals from the organ to make a sound. The way in which the signals are produced varies from one organ to another. Some organs have metal discs or tone wheels with teeth or wavy lines cut into them. Electric motors drive the discs, and pickups like those in electric guitars produce electric signals as the discs rotate. Pressing a key allows the signal for that note to go to the amplifier. Other organs have metal reeds that vibrate instead of rotating discs, while some have electronic components that produce signals without any moving parts. These electronic organs are like synthesizers.

Laurens Hammond, the inventor of the electric organ, also invented an automatic transmission, a 'tickless' clock, 3-dimensional movies, and a sugar-refining process.

Right: A modern Hammond organ, showing its two manuals, drawbars and stops, as well as foot pedals and swell control. In 1937 the US Federal Trade Commission objected to the claim that these instruments were organs. So a test was arranged at the Rockefeller Chapel of Chicago University. The speakers of a Hammond organ were hidden amongst the pipes of the chapel organ, and with both players hidden, 15 students and 15 musicians tried to tell which was which. For 33% of the time they were wrong, and the case was dropped!

Organ sounds

A pipe organ has sets of stops which control different sets of pipes with various tone qualities. An electric organ has sets of buttons which control the instrument to produce a similar range of sounds.

The pitch of notes is usually referred to by the numbers two, four, eight and sixteen and the higher the number the lower the note. This is based on the pipe length in a pipe organ, where longer (sixteen foot) pipes make lower notes.

But in addition to this the electric organ has a set of drawbars by the keyboard which alter the tone, and the player can choose different combinations of drawbars to get different sounds. The drawbars are also marked with numbers up to sixteen. In addition, many organists used a Leslie speaker, which has rotating loudspeakers to give a special sound.

Playing the electric organ

Many people enjoy playing an electric organ because its range of sounds makes it rather like having an orchestra of your own. As well as stops and drawbars, the organ may have two keyboards or manuals to give two sounds at the same time, foot pedals arranged as a keyboard for bass notes, and an automatic rhythm unit that produces drum and percussion rhythms as accompaniment.

Playing an organ is not like playing the piano, because the notes stop immediately the keys are released. The fingers have to be kept on the keys for as long as the notes are required to sound. There is another foot pedal to make the sound louder or softer, and pressing the pedal gradually gives the music a dramatic swell.

Synthesizers

What happens to a sound?

A synthesizer is an electronic instrument, and makes no sound of its own. It uses electronic components to produce electric signals which turn into sounds when sent through an amplifier to a loudspeaker. A synthesizer is able to make up a range of sounds, and this usually includes imitations of other instruments as well as sounds of its own, and non-musical sounds like a roaring wind.

The way the instrument works is connected with every sound we hear. Every sound has a beginning, a middle and an end: an attack, a sustain and a decay time. This is true of a short sound like a slamming door or a long sound like a ship's hooter. These three stages, attack, sustain and decay, are well demonstrated by a note played on a xylophone. It is also possible to make a graph of what happens.

Attack: The note is begun by the sharp sound of the beater hitting the xylophone bar.

Sustain: As the note sounds, it reverberates and sustains, helped by its resonator.

Decay: As the note starts to die away, it reverberates less, decays and stops.

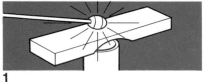

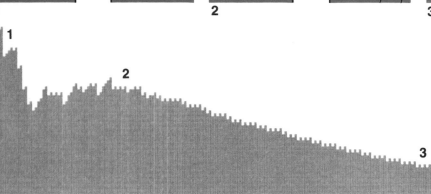

Envelopes

When all three stages (attack, sustain and decay time) are taken together, they produce a way of looking at a sound that is rather like taking its fingerprint. The same note played on a piano and then a trumpet will have a completely different attack, sustain and decay. It is this which makes any sound distinctive, and the combination – a sound from beginning to end – is called an envelope. What the synthesizer does is to give the player control over the envelopes of sound made by the instrument, by separating the stages.

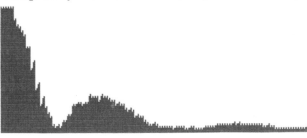

The envelope of a piano

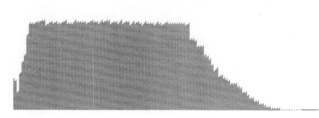

The envelope of a trumpet

The keyboard shown across the centre of this page is a typical modern synthesizer, with a small keyboard, and all the other controls carefully grouped in sections with labels. All synthesizers have the envelope generator, tone generator and filters in common.

Looking at a synthesizer

Synthesizers can be played with a keyboard, blown, plucked or hit (all these types are described on the next page), but they all combine two different types of control. The keyboard part (to take the most common type) is used to select what note or notes will be played. The other controls are used to decide what sort of notes they are going to be. They follow a simple sequence, from making a simple sound, through giving it a distinctive 'envelope' to filtering out any parts of it that will not be amplified. The three parts of this sequence relate to the three main types of synthesizer control, although most synthesizers have various other types of control as well.

The envelope generator is on the top right labelled EG. As well as attack, sustain and decay sliders, there is a release slider which controls when the sound of a note stops.
The VCO is the tone generator or oscillator. The wave form controls affect the type of note produced. In the centre is the filter or VCF, which allows the player to cut out some pitches, and to control echo with the resonance control. Volume is controlled by the knob on the left.

The envelope generator. This has the controls to allow a player to decide on the attack, sustain and decay times of all the notes played.

The tone generator. Usually the sound itself is generated by an oscillator. This produces electrical signals, which, when played straight through an amplifier give a pure and smooth electronic sound, rather like the test tuning signal on a radio or television. The faster it produces its signal, the higher the note, and an oscillator can be controlled so that notes can be produced exactly using the pitch control. The loudness of the note is determined by the amplitude control, or by a separate volume control.

The filter. After the player has pressed a key on the keyboard, the oscillator produced a note and the envelope generator given it an attack, sustain and decay time, it passes through a filter, which cuts out or increases some frequencies of the note. This controls the tone quality of the note.

Different types of synthesizer

Andy Mackay plays a blown synthesizer

Below: The Minimoog has long been the most popular small synthesizer. The wheels at the side of the keyboard enable the player to bend the pitch of the notes and glide between them, producing a strong solo style.

Digital or analog?

Where the sound made by a synthesizer is produced as electric signals from an oscillator, it is known as an analog synthesizer, but more recent varieties use the digital memory of a computer as the source of signals, which will produce a bigger and more flexible range of sounds when put through a speaker and amplifier.

Monophonic synthesizers

Many synthesizers, especially the less expensive instruments, are monophonic. This means that they only produce one note at a time – as a flute or trumpet does. However, this is not necessarily a disadvantage because it leaves one hand free to operate the synthesizer controls while the other plays the keyboard.

Most monophonic synthesizers are small keyboard instruments, easy to place on a larger instrument such as an electric piano. Although the keyboard is small – usually only three octaves wide – the synthesizers have a switch to change the range of the keyboard and get high or low notes.

Not all synthesizers are operated by keyboards. There are synthesizers which are blown, with a special mouthpiece that produces an electric signal. The keys are played like the keys on a woodwind instrument, and they change the signal to produce different notes from the synthesizer.

Many drummers like to expand the sounds of their drum kit with percussion synthesizers. These synthesizers look like small drums, and are hit with a stick to produce a sound.

Some guitar synthesizers do not even have strings, but use touch-sensitive pads between the frets. Other synthesizer controls are on the body of the instrument in place of the electric guitar's tone and volume knobs.

Below: Jean-Michel Jarre playing a group of synthesizers

Polyphonic synthesizers

Several kinds of synthesizers can produce chords when more than one key is pressed down at the same time. These synthesizers are called polyphonic synthesizers. Some of them have touch-sensitive keys like a piano and the sound varies depending on how hard the keys are struck. However, like most monophonic synthesizers, the less expensive polyphonic synthesizers do not have the touch-sensitive keys. Playing them is rather like playing an organ.

Changing sounds can be a problem with polyphonic synthesizers since both hands are used to play the keyboard. Many of them therefore have buttons which, when pressed, change the sound instantly. In several instruments, the sounds are set by the manufacturer. But some synthesizers contain an electronic memory that stores a whole range of control settings fed in by the player.

Another kind of synthesizer is for use by guitarists. Instead of having a keyboard, it has strings and is played like a guitar, and the sound that comes out can be controlled like that of any synthesizer.

Perhaps the most amazing of all electronic instruments is the vocoder which is connected both to a microphone and a synthesizer. The singer sings into the microphone but the actual pitches that come out of the vocoder are controlled by notes played on a keyboard. If the synthesizer is polyphonic a whole choir will emerge from the vocoder!

In the studio

Rock band Yazoo using a synthesizer in part of an elaborate stage set

Below: A typical synthesizer recording studio used by composer Vangelis

Although synthesizers are used in rock bands for live performances, there is also an enormous amount of synthesizer music produced by the process of recording and mixing. Using a 24-track tape recorder and one synthesizer, a single musician can build up a piece of music, recording one sound after another.

This can be difficult, especially at the beginning when there are no other sounds to play with. The first sound that is recorded is therefore usually a click track, which sounds like a metronome, or an automatic synthesizer rhythm. The musician keeps time by listening to the click track or rhythm, which is removed later when it is no longer needed.

Conventional instruments can be synthesized and their sound mixed with electronic effects only possible with a synthesizer. All the sounds are then mixed together, transferred to a final tape and the result is a whole orchestra of synthesizers.

Vangelis constructing a film soundtrack, as he did for *Blade Runner*

Below: The BBC Radiophonic workshop has produced electronic music for many years.

Some synthesizer musicians use synthesizers to imitate instruments of the orchestra, making synthesized versions of pieces written by classical composers. These can be very effective if done well, but are very different from the original piece of music, because in order to record the layers of sound one after another, the musicians have to keep to a very strict rhythm never found in classical music, which is always speeding up and slowing down slightly. In a performance of an orchestral work, each player contributes something individual to the music which a single synthesizer musician cannot hope to match.

Other synthesizer players use studios and tape recorders to produce original compositions, often for soundtracks to films, commercials and television programmes, and as backings for pop records. Many film companies and broadcasting stations maintain their own electronic studios to produce music for soundtracks.

Electronic instruments

Above: Youseff Yancy with a modern version of the theremin

Below: Jeanne Loriod playing the ondes martenot in a performance of the *Turangalîla Symphony* by Olivier Messiaen. Behind her are the loudspeakers which amplify the sounds of the instrument, played with her right hand and controlled with her left.

The first people to think about making music electronically were composers in the early years of this century searching for new sounds. As early as 1906 a vast electronic instrument was built which produced sounds from dynamos (electric generators) transmitting them over telephone wires. It weighed 200 tonnes and was later dismantled so we cannot tell today what it sounded like.

Most successful electronic instruments were designed after 1915 when the invention of electronic valves made oscillators and amplifiers possible. In 1920 the theremin (named after its inventor, Léon Thérémin) was first demonstrated. Sounds were made by the player's hands waving around a metal rod and loop. This produced an eerie tone, and a glissando effect which was often used in science fiction films.

In 1928 two electronic instruments were invented that were more advanced – the ondes martenot and the trautonium. Only the ondes martenot can still be heard today. It consists of a keyboard which controls an oscillator, an amplifier and a loudspeaker. Only one note can be produced at a time but the sound quality of the note can be varied by controls operated by the left hand. The keys also move slightly from side to side, producing a *vibrato*, or wobble in the pitch of the note. The ondes martenot makes a sound similar to the human voice and is used in *Trois Petites Liturgies* by Messiaen.

A performance of a tape piece,
Futuristie 1 by Pierre Henry

The tape recorder

The tape recorder, invented in 1935, is not strictly a musical instrument. It makes no sound of its own, but records and plays back sounds fed into it. If these sounds are assembled on tape and then played back, it can be thought of as an instrument.

It has been used to make music in many different ways. The first of these was in the very early 1950s when a Frenchman, Pierre Schaeffer, started to compose what he called *musique concrete* – music made out of recordings of all kinds of different noises from railway trains to a piano. The sounds are 'treated' – slowed down, speeded up, played backwards or broken down into tiny fragments – so that they are unrecognisable as everyday noises. They are turned into new sounds which can be extremely high or low, sharp and attacking or slow-moving and soothing.

To produce this kind of music all that is needed is two good tape recorders which can record and play back at different speeds. One is used to hold the tape on which the original material has been recorded (and absolutely any sounds can be used) and the other to transfer the sounds on to at the speed and in the order required.

It is also possible to splice the tape itself – chopping it up and sticking it back together in a different order.

Right: A studio tape recorder, known as reel to reel, as the tape is held in the large metal spools. It records in four channels, each monitored by one of the meters at the bottom.

Electronic music

Because electronic sounds are projected out of loudspeakers it is possible to make them move around in space. Loudspeakers can be attached to, or suspended from, walls and ceilings, and the sounds can be made to travel across the room by using the speakers selectively. Several composers have written pieces to be performed in a particular building with a specific arrangement of speakers. Iannis Xenakis, who trained as an architect, composed *Concret P-H* for the Philips Pavilion at the Brussels World Fair in 1958, in which 350 loudspeakers were used.

Shortly after *musique concrète* was first produced in Paris, various composers grouped together in Germany and started to create what they called *Elektronische Musik*. The tape recorder was essential to record the sound material and perform the music, but with this kind of music a lot of the sounds were produced electronically.

This was before synthesizers were invented, and composers like Karlheinz Stockhausen spent up to a year and a half putting together one piece of music. They had oscillators which produced different pitches, but these all sounded much the same – very smooth and pure. To make different sounds, several of these pure sounds – called *sine waves* – had to be recorded over the top of each other. It could take all day to build up one sound which might only be needed for a few seconds.

A pitched note, played on an instrument like the piano, contains a whole range of these simple sounds in the relationship known as the *harmonic series*. However, in one of his first electronic pieces, *Studie II* (1959–60), Stockhausen built 'new', unpitched sounds by adding sine waves together in different ways. Stockhausen was trying to encourage a new way of listening in which it was not the pitch of the noise that was important, but the particular quality of the sound.

Karlheinz Stockhausen rehearsing his piece *Sirius*, in which the sound of the trumpet (played by his son) is picked up by a microphone and altered electronically

In 1624 Francis Bacon, writing about a future world, seems to have foreseen electronic music. 'We also have Sound-houses, where we practise and demonstrate all Sounds, and their Generation . . . We make diverse Tremblings and Warblings of Sounds . . . We also have means to convey Sounds . . . in strange Lines and Distances.'
The New Atlantis

A rehearsal of Berio's *Laborintus II*, conducted by the composer. The three people in the foreground are controlling the tape recorder and mixing desk.

Performing electronic music

Tape music is unlike any other kind of music in that it doesn't need a performer to interpret it. There is only one version of the piece – the one put together by the composer.

In some pieces, however, instrumentalists play at the same time as tape-recorded music. Close coordination between the two is essential, and the performers have to play at exactly the right speed and keep in time with the recording, because whereas humans can adjust to each other's interpretation of the music, the tape recorder is inflexible.

Another way of involving electronic techniques and performers live on the stage is to pick up the sounds of the instruments on a microphone. Instruments are amplified in all kinds of music, but it is also possible to alter their sound. This is what happens in Stockhausen's *Mikrophonie I* (1964). Two performers play a large tam-tam, stroking and beating it to make as many different sounds as possible. Two performers operate the microphones transferring the sound to the electronic equipment which is operated by two more.

John Cage wrote several pieces for electronic instruments, to be performed on stage. As in all his music many of the decisions about how to play the music are left to the performers. In *Imaginary Landscape no. 3* six musicians play on both percussion instruments and electronic equipment. There are no pitches written down, only *glissandos* – slides through the notes, either up or down.

Computers

Top: Programming a music computer using the keyboard

Above: Alterations being made to a music programme using a light pen on the screen

Below: A portable synthesizer with a programmable memory

The computer is affecting and changing many human activities, and music is no exception. There are many ways in which a computer can be used to make music, but all, of course, depend on the instructions fed into the machine by a human programmer. One of the most obvious ways of using a computer is as a memory. A sound can be created, fed into the computer and easily recalled when needed. This can be seen on the simplest of synthesizers, operated by a microchip. The musician changes from one kind of sound to another with the flick of a switch.

Much more powerful computers exist which have not only vast memories, but the ability to create almost any sound imaginable. Data is fed in by the programmer, either as a series of numbers, or through a keyboard similar to that of a synthesizer. The sounds which are produced can be made to appear in different forms on the visual display unit (VDU). It is then possible to alter the sounds by making adjustments to the waveforms shown on the VDU with a light pen.

This kind of computer can also cope with data fed in as sound. It analyses the noise, reducing it to a series of digits, and can then either reproduce it or change it. Using everyday sounds in this way, composers can create a kind of *musique concrète* with much more scope than old-fashioned tape splicing. To make a taped sound higher, for example, the tape has to be played faster. The sound lasts for a shorter length of time, and is also distorted. The computer can synthesize the sound at any pitch, without changing it, for as long as required. One of the simplest exercises is to take a dog's bark and make a tune out of it. More serious uses of this technique have involved voices and acoustic instruments, and often the synthesized sounds and the recorded sounds are mixed in such a way that it is difficult to tell the difference.

Taped electronic music is often felt to be inhuman and unnatural. This is partly because a performer cannot be seen, and it is difficult to work out where the sounds are coming from or how they are made. But recently it has become possible to use a computer together with live performers.

Normally, when a computer is used to compose music, there is a time delay of several minutes between the programming of the machine and the production of the sound. Now, a very sophisticated computer has been made which computes in 'real time'. There is no delay between when a sound is requested and when it comes out of the loudspeakers.

One way in which this computer can be used, for example, is for a single note played on an instrument and picked up by a microphone to be transformed into a whole sequence of different notes. If a second note is played before the first sequence has ended, a second, overlapping sequence is created. In this way, whole 'clouds' of sound can be produced, and of course the programme can be changed to bring in new sequences.

Although this kind of music can be composed and stored on tape to be replayed at a performance, the advantage of a real-time computer is that several performers can play together and the piece of music will sound slightly different each time it is performed.

In a recent piece by Pierre Boulez called *Répons* (response), six soloists are connected to a computer, while a chamber orchestra, which is not treated electronically, performs with them. The conductor is able to control all the elements, including the building up of sound patterns created by the computer.

This use of the computer has yet to be fully developed, and is still very complicated and expensive to set up. But as the technology for producing electronic music becomes more developed, the possibilities of the composer and performer actually achieving the sounds they want, and controlling their production, become greater.

Boulez conducting a rehearsal of *Répons*. The sounds of some of the instruments are altered by a computer, which is controlled by technicians operating the terminals.

Technicians and equipment involved in a performance of *Répons*. The leads coming from the terminals are connected to the computer and to microphones picking up the instruments' sounds.

Above: Laurie Anderson, the American musician who uses electronic equipment in an original way, and combines it with dramatic lighting and other special effects.

Above: In this studio, a synthesizer player (foreground) is having his music mixed (centre) with sounds produced by the saxophonist beyond the glass in the far wall.

Below: The German rock band Kraftwerk in performance. They use synthesizers to produce music concerned mainly with the subjects of industry and technology.

Composing, performing, recording

1 composer
2 conductor
3 music librarian
4 orchestral attendant
5 record producer
6 sound engineer

As well as the instrumentalists, singers and electronic equipment involved in making music, it could not be performed or reproduced without many of the people shown on this page. A piece of music goes through many processes: from composition through to rehearsal, performance, publication, and often broadcast or recording. But at the end of a performance the audience tends to applaud only the people actually seen and heard – the people on the stage – and to forget about all the people working behind the scenes.

The composer

Parental encouragement from the composer Elizabeth Maconchy for her daughter Nicola LeFanu, also famous as a composer

Below: The young Mozart was encouraged to play the harpsichord and violin, and to compose. He and his sister were taken by his father to courts all over Europe to show off their skills. Here is Mozart at the court of the Empress Maria Theresa.

No-one can explain why certain people feel the need to write music. There must be people who would be able to compose, given the opportunity (just as there are people who do write music which nobody else thinks is any good). Early encouragement helps would-be composers to get started, but many have persevered against opposition from their families which perhaps even strengthened their determination.

Not many composers, if asked why they compose, are able to explain very clearly. But often there is a need to communicate with other people in a way not possible with words. A composer may use musical 'language' to arouse emotions in people but whereas a story-teller might describe a happy or sad event by using appropriate words, when the language is rhythm, harmony and melody, the emotions are harder to define. Not all composers set out to arouse emotion, or to express it – as not all listeners are moved in the same way by the same piece of music – but the joy of composing is putting together the ingredients of the musical language in a way which is both original and also makes sense to the listener.

The art of composition lies in the skill with which melody, harmony and tone colours are put together. The composer uses music to express ideas which can sometimes be part of a broader artistic or philosophical movement. As we identify painting or poetry as, for example, Classical, Romantic or Expressionist, so we can associate the music of certain composers with these movements.

The two Hungarian composers Bartók and Kodály, in 1912. They worked together on methods of collecting and writing down folk-songs and were also great friends, each giving the other advice and criticism on their music.

Olivier Messiaen, born at the beginning of this century, with some of his pupils. He has a great reputation as a teacher and held classes in eastern Europe and America, as well as teaching in Paris for 20 years.

Right: Sir Edward Elgar at work on an orchestral score. He wrote his first piece at the age of 10 but had no formal music lessons. He taught himself to compose by performing and listening to other people's music.

Is it possible to teach composition?

Many composers argue that composition cannot really be taught, and point out that certain great composers, such as Elgar, never had a composition lesson in their lives. This is partly true. Composition can only be learnt by actually composing. But what the young composer needs, as well as knowing about how to write down or notate music, is an experienced mind to react against – someone who can listen and advise. A good teacher acts as a mirror in which the student's ideas are reflected more critically and clearly. The best test of any new composition, though, is a performance, when a level of artistic interpretation is added to the composer's work.

Many composers learn to compose by imitating the music they most admire. Others think their music is entirely original and only realize later how influenced they are by music they have listened to. Even so, it is possible to learn, without imitation, from the ways previous composers have overcome certain problems, such as how to make all the musical ideas fit together – how to structure a piece of music. And of course a composer gains experience from his or her own mistakes: a process of learning which can last a lifetime.

Many composers began young. Mozart started to compose at the age of five and was very accomplished by the time he was ten. But even he had to copy someone, and it was many years before he developed a way of saying things which was entirely his own.

'Never compose anything unless the not composing of it becomes a positive nuisance to you.'
Gustav Holst (above)

'Composing is like driving down a foggy road toward a house. Slowly you see more details of the house – the colour of the slates and bricks, the shape of the windows. The notes are the bricks and mortar of the house.'
Benjamin Britten

Right: As well as writing in trains or cars, Duke Ellington, the jazz composer, would write in his dressing room between appearances on stage with his band. Here he is working out instrumental parts from the piano score of a song.

Inspiration

Ideas for a composition seem to come in different ways. Sometimes they arrive in the shape of an actual tune, or a sequence of harmonies, and the composer will feel that they will become a certain kind of composition. The textures may seem right for a string quartet or a piano sonata, or the idea may already suggest a particular instrument or instrumental combination. Other composers have a general idea of the shape a new work will take when it is finished. They can glimpse its outline before knowing what the details are to be.

The idea of hearing music inside one's head might seem strange and almost impossible. But it is no more strange than reading the words of a printed page and 'hearing' them in one's mind at the same time – something we can all do. A composer has to know not only how written notes sound when they are played, but also the particular tones of all the instruments, played on their own and in different combinations. On reading a score the music can then be heard in the mind quite clearly.

The process can also be reversed so that the correct notation will be used to write down music composed in the imagination. The memory is trained by reading scores and listening intently to performances.

Composers have tried in all kinds of ways to stimulate their imaginations. Some, like Beethoven, have found inspiration in country walks. Mozart, on the other hand, found that a game of billiards sometimes helped to encourage the flow of ideas. Benjamin Britten, like the jazz composer Duke Ellington, often planned his music while in a car or train. But this is only the beginning of a piece of music. It can't be written while playing billiards, and the next step involves hours at a desk with pen or pencil and manuscript paper.

The composer John McCabe sometimes starts to compose a piece by describing it in words. He may then wait for several months before writing the music, giving the idea time to work itself out in his head.

'When I write lyrics, I write music and lyrics together. And not at the piano, but when I'm walking along the street. That's the time to polish off a phrase, when you're walking and its sings well, naturally.'
Billy Strayhorn

Mozart composed very rapidly in his head, and relied on his phenomenal memory, as he told his father: 'Today we had a concert, where three of my compositions were performed, including a sonata with violin accompaniment for myself, which I composed last night between eleven and twelve (but in order to be able to finish it, I only wrote out the accompaniment for Brunetti and retained my own part in my head).'

Right: Sketches by Stravinsky for *The Rite of Spring*. Some of the ideas are only one bar long, and some are only rhythms without pitches.

How do composers work?

There seems to be no single method of composition shared by all composers, but they all need one thing: a stretch of uninterrupted time. Many, it seems, like to work fixed hours each day. Some prefer to work in the early evening and some at night for the sake of the extra peace and quiet. But whatever the time of day the point is the regularity of the routine. It is only through self-discipline that the work will get done.

Some composers like to work out their musical ideas on paper, making endless sketches, altering each phrase until it reaches a perfect and satisfying shape. Beethoven worked in this way, and many of his sketchbooks survive in museums from which we can follow the process in fascinating detail. Others prefer to carry out the same process almost entirely in their heads, only putting their thoughts on paper when they have been finally shaped. Mozart often worked in this way, and so, more recently, did Benjamin Britten.

Some composers find it helpful to test out their ideas on a piano as they go along – Haydn did, and Stravinsky. Others, like Berlioz, have scorned the idea of gaining help from the keyboard (he could not play the piano anyway!) claiming that it actually inhibits the flow of musical thought. But even if a composer does use the piano it is not merely to fish around for ideas. The mind is in control and not the fingers. The sound of the music helps to stimulate the imagination.

> 'When I am asked to compose a work for an occasion, great or small, I want to know in some detail the conditions of the place where it will be performed, the size and acoustics, what instruments will be available and suitable, the kind of people who will hear it, and what language they will understand – and even sometimes the age of the listeners and performers.'
> Benjamin Britten

Right: Frederick the Great (playing the flute) employed several musicians, including C P E Bach and Quantz (on the far right) who wrote 300 flute concertos for him.

Below: One kind of organization to commission new music is a television company. Here we see a scene from Benjamin Britten's opera *Owen Wingrave* which was commissioned by BBC television.

How do composers earn a living?

Sometimes a composer does not know what to write until someone actually asks for a particular piece of music. Only then do the ideas begin to flow. This practice of commissioning a piece of music has a long history. Many of the masterpieces of the past have come about in this way.

In the eighteenth century, composers were often employed full-time to write music on a regular basis and for special occasions. Haydn worked as a paid servant of the Esterházy princes, writing all the music required for the daily activities of the palace: operas, church music, symphonies, chamber music. Since the beginning of the last century, however, composers have usually made a living from individuals or organizations commissioning pieces on a one-time basis. Nowadays commissions tend to come from festival committees, symphony societies, orchestras and well-known performing artists rather than wealthy private individuals.

Part of Beethoven's finished manuscript for his ninth symphony, composed between 1821 and 1824. From this, the copyist had to produce a neat version which the performers could use.

'When I first wrote down music I didn't do it very well. I'm left-handed, and I always seemed to have my hand smudging the page. But gradually I came to feel that making a score look good – look beautiful, look very clear and easy for the performer – was a very important part of being a composer.'
Nicola LeFanu

Right: An extract from the published score of a piece by Nicola LeFanu, taken from the composer's original manuscript

The completed manuscript

The first form a newly finished piece of orchestral music takes is usually a detailed sketch to be played on the piano, or a full score with all the instrumental parts written out separately underneath each other. If a sketch, or piano score, is used, it will have to be worked up into a full score at the next stage of composition. It is likely that these early versions of the work have been jotted down very quickly and are not easy for anyone but the composer to read. Such a score would be useless to a performer and so the composer must either prepare a clean score that can be read with ease, or hand over the manuscript to a professional copyist to do the job.

Nowadays most young composers make a point of learning how to write their scores in a neat, legible hand. This is partly a matter of professional pride, and partly economic necessity, for the work of a copyist is skilled and must be paid for at an appropriate rate. But there have been great composers whose manuscripts are almost impossible to decipher: Beethoven, Puccini, Janáček, and Vaughan Williams among them.

Copying out a composer's manuscript is not simply a question of transferring the notes on to another sheet of paper. Careful planning is needed. Often separate parts will be required for each instrument, as well as a full score. Not every instrument is being asked to play all the time, and long passages where the instrument is not required are indicated by a single number equivalent to the numbers of bars' rest. Often, after several bars' rest, 'cues' must be put in – showing a part that is being played by another instrument – so that the player can locate the new entry precisely. It is also important for the copyist to make sure that the music reaches the bottom of the page at a convenient point for the player to turn over – one that doesn't interfere with the music.

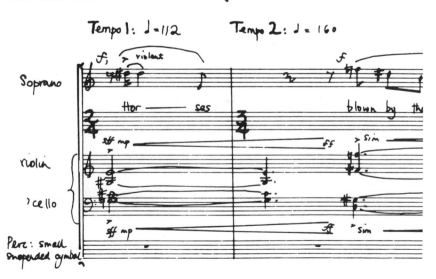

The conductor

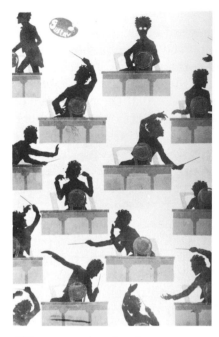

Silhouettes showing the gestures of Gustav Mahler (1860–1911) when conducting. Best known today as a composer, conducting took up a large part of his life.

However beautifully written, a score is not actually the music itself, but only a series of instructions which have to be obeyed in order for the music to become sound. The composer's finished work needs an interpreter to turn it into sound. Chief among the interpreters of music is the conductor.

Historically, the conductor is a late arrival on the musical scene. In the eighteenth century, when orchestras were small and compact, performances were often directed either by the principal violinist or by someone sitting at a harpsichord who completed the harmony by playing the appropriate chords. When orchestras began to increase in size, and the music they played became more complex, it was necessary to have a person giving directions as to how the music should be played. By the middle of the nineteenth century, the conductor had become an essential part of the musical scene.

In some respects the conductor has to be the most complete, all-round musician of all the performers. To be a conductor it is not necessary to be able to play every instrument, but it is essential to have a thorough understanding of their capabilities and the techniques involved in playing them. Not only must the conductor be able to read music, but a deep appreciation of every type of music is also important, since that of one period demands a different approach to that of another.

Pierre Boulez, the French composer and conductor, who does not use a baton to direct the orchestra

The American, Leonard Bernstein, always a dramatic conductor, also a world-famous composer

There are two main tools of the conductor's trade: the ear and the power to communicate, through hand gestures and facial expression, with every member of the orchestra. The conductor must hear the slightest error in the playing of the notes, supply all the details of a performance and take the final responsibility for the interpretation of the composer's score. It is in this that the conductor's integrity rests.

Although an orchestral score will give instructions for performance it can never be absolutely precise. For example, in a loud passage the instrumentalists will be instructed to play *forte* (loudly). But exactly how loud is *forte*? The strength of sound coming from a trombone playing at this level will be much greater than that of a flute. The composer may try to put right such problems by indicating, for instance, that the different instruments play at different volumes, but it will still be up to the conductor to make the final decision, and arrive at the best balance.

There is also the matter of speed. The composer may ask for a movement to be played *allegro* (in a lively way), and may even supply a metronome mark indicating so many beats per minute. But the conductor will know that the composer will not expect every bar to be taken at the same relentless pace. The music must be allowed to ebb and flow slightly – allowed to breathe – so that it does not become mechanical and rigid.

Seiji Ozawa conducts opera, as well as the Boston Symphony Orchestra.

Simon Rattle, one of the youngest professional conductors in the world today

The editor, André Previn, conducting an orchestral concert

The orchestra

Soloists involved in an orchestral work – such as a pianist in a piano concerto – may only join the orchestra for the last two rehearsals. They will then work out with the conductor the final details of interpretation, and the speed the music should be played. They rehearse passages which may cause problems.

Right: André Previn discussing a score with the manager of the LSO in 1973, Harold Lawrence

Orchestral rehearsals

Rehearsals can take place at any time of day and last up to three hours. For most concerts it may be necessary to have three or four such sessions – more if a new or difficult work is to be performed.

Before the rehearsal the conductor will have studied the score minutely and thought about the way in which it should be played. The aim of the rehearsal is to convey to the orchestra the conductor's interpretation of the music and this will usually be done by taking the music to pieces; passages will be repeated and individual sections of the orchestra will be asked to play separately. By the end, all the players should know in what way their individual parts contribute to the overall effect of the music.

A rehearsal for a piece by Stockhausen in which some of the players are required to act

Right: The composer and conductor Andrzej Panufnik discussing a passage in his music with a percussionist

A player, only required for a few minutes of a lengthy rehearsal, occupies himself while not playing

Below: The conductor Pierre Boulez discussing the orchestra's rehearsal schedule with its concert master or leader

Orchestral administration

The orchestra does not consist of the conductor and players alone. Behind the scenes is an administrative staff to take care of its day-to-day running. There is a librarian to take charge of the music and put it out on the music stands before each performance. This has to be done very carefully because it would be easy to get the parts mixed up and put them on the wrong stands. The librarian is also responsible for checking parts for accuracy and erasing markings which are not wanted. Orchestral attendants take charge of the music stands and seats, and shift such cumbersome instruments as pianos and double basses. Usually an accountant and a general manager oversee the entire enterprise.

These are just some of the staff involved in running a full-time orchestra, whose annual routine will include not only regular concerts, but tours within its home country and abroad, and recording sessions for films and gramophone records, all of which have to be planned to the last minute and in elaborate detail.

Conductors are also involved in administration, particularly the 'principal' conductor or Music Director. One of the most important jobs is to audition new players when vacancies occur. The orchestra's programme – what, where and when it is going to perform – also has to be planned, and guest conductors and soloists must be chosen. The Music Director is involved in all these operations.

Vocal music

The répétiteur and chorus master Nina Walker has a particular way of rehearsing singers and choirs: 'When I teach a singer a new operatic role, I always start with the characterization. The libretto (the words) must come first – just as it does with the composer. When I'm preparing a new work with a choir I do exactly the same. I like the choir to understand the work as drama first, and then go on to see how the composer has interpreted the words in the music.'

A rehearsal of the London Symphony Orchestra and Chorus conducted by their chorus master Richard Hickox.

Chorus master

As well as using an orchestra, a lot of music performed in concert halls involves a chorus and solo singers. Frequently, although the soloists are professional singers, the members of the chorus are not full-time musicians but only come together to rehearse in their spare time. They are trained and rehearsed by a chorus master, whose duties involve teaching the chorus the music they are to perform, as well as working to make them into a unified body which sings with one voice.

Most chorus masters conduct their own choirs in some concerts, but often the choir is seen as part of an orchestra and for the final rehearsals and the actual performance another, orchestral, conductor will take over.

The répétiteur

The répétiteur (the word is French and means 'coach') works in an opera house, accompanying singers and helping them to remember both the words and the music. The conductor of an opera might only arrive at a late stage of rehearsal, and until that time it is the répétiteur who gives advice on musical interpretation. An experienced répétiteur knows roughly how each conductor will want the music performed.

Because an opera company hires singers of many nationalities, répétiteurs have to work in several languages, French, German and Italian being the most likely.

A view of the inside of a prompt box. During a performance the conductor would be shown on the television screen.

In the opera house, one of the répétiteur's duties is to appear in the prompt box – a small room set into the front of the stage low enough so that only the occupant's head is visible, and then only from the stage itself. Here the répétiteur sits during the performance, following the score and speaking the opening words of each entry in the rhythm to which it will be sung while at the same time indicating with the right hand the exact moment when the singer is to come in. Although the singers have memorised their parts it is important to have this safety measure as a moment's hesitation on the part of the singer could be disastrous with the conductor a long way away, separated from the stage by the orchestra.

If the répétiteur is not on duty in the prompt box, he or she may be called upon to conduct any instrumentalists or singers who have to play off-stage. This happens fairly often in operas when the composer has asked for such things as chiming bells, thunder claps, or choruses singing without being seen. Obviously it is not possible for the people who are playing or singing to see the conductor (without peering round the scenery, which would look rather comic) so the répétiteur acts as an extension of the conductor and gives them their cue.

Below: A rehearsal involving two singers on the stage of London's Royal Opera House. The répétiteur is at the piano.

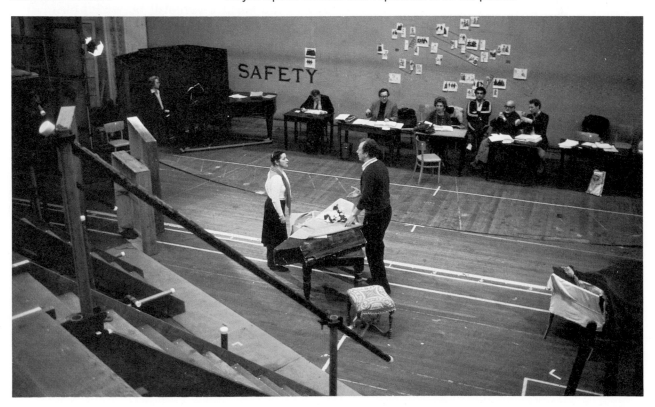

Music printing

Engraving a phrase mark. The notes can be made by punching – hitting a special tool with a hammer to mark the notes – but other marks are drawn freehand.

Before any piece of music can be printed, the manuscript must be turned into a form from which a printer's plate can be made. In general, there are two different systems by which this is done. In the first, skilled craftsmen make up the actual plate itself which will be used for printing, and this will either be by engraving a metal plate or preparing a thin stone plate for lithography. In the second, various methods are used to make a perfect copy of the finished page, which is then photographed, and the film used to make a printing plate. These methods include stencilling, 'dry-transfer' letterings, the music typewriter, and now, the music-setting computer.

Engraving

The music engraver makes a printing plate by carefully scratching a sheet of copper. All the lines of the stave are ruled out, and the notes put in either by stamps, by stencil or freehand. But all this has to be done back to front, as if in a mirror. This is because, when the plate comes to be printed, the shallow recesses in the plate are filled up with ink. The flat surface is then wiped clean, and when the inked plate is pressed against paper, the paper is printed with a negative of the pattern on the plate, so, in order that the music is the right way round the plate must be scratched in reverse. Mistakes have to be polished out and rescratched, so that the recesses for ink join up, and the surface can still be wiped clean.

Lithography

A lithographic plate is made by roughly the same principle as engraving, only the music is written on to a stone with wax. The stone is then dipped into an acid bath, and the unwaxed parts are eaten away, leaving the notes as a raised part of the stone. These are then inked and printed, but it is the *raised* surfaces, not the depressions, that hold the ink.

Pulling a piece of paper from the metal plate. The music comes out the right way round.

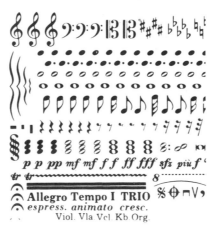

Dry-transfer music setting showing (above) how it is done, and (left) a transfer sheet

Stencilling

When music is stencilled, the effect produced is that of a large-scale picture of the eventual printed page. The artist works at a larger size than the final page so that mistakes can be more easily corrected, and the results photographically reduced. The five-line staves are rolled on with a special parallel pen, and the notes, signs and symbols are stencilled through brass cut-outs of their shapes.

Dry transfer

In this system, a 'same-size' picture of the finished music is produced. The stave is generally drawn on paper as with stencilling, using a parallel pen, and the notes are supplied on the back of a transparent plastic sheet. By gently rubbing the top of the sheet, the note is transferred to the paper.

Music typewriter

The typewriter can only type music in one size, so any changes in size between the typed sheet and the eventual printed page must be done photographically. Pressing the keys produces notes and symbols instead of letters. The roller of the typewriter does not shift after each key is pressed, as with a normal typewriter, and the operator carefully repositions the carriage for each new note. Music typewriters are faster, but perhaps less accurate than stencilling or dry transfer.

Computer setting

This is done with a combination of a music typewriter and a piano keyboard, that displays its results on a television screen. The operator types in the music, and the computer's memory stores it. Simple corrections can be made on to the screen itself with a light pen, or by retyping sections of the music into the machine.

The machine produces a large-sized 'proof' of its work for rechecking, which is done on tracing paper by an electronically-controlled pen. Copies of this can be sent to the composer or copyist for them to spot mistakes, and again these can be retyped on the keyboard. Eventually, the machine makes a piece of finished film of the music which can be used to manufacture a printing plate.

A music typewriter. Although outwardly like a normal typewriter, it has notes and signs instead of letters on its keys.

The computer setter. A note is selected with the buttons on the left and made to appear on the screen with one of the buttons on the right.

Ownership of music

Copyright

Nowadays the legal owner of the copyright of a piece of music is the composer, who holds the right to print, publish, or sell copies of the work, perform or record it.

Legal recognition of such ownership did not always exist. In Mozart's day it was common practice for copyists to sell pirated copies of the works they had been engaged to reproduce, and unscrupulous publishers would print them without the composer's permission, and without handing over any of the profits.

During the nineteenth and twentieth centuries, laws were passed which protected the composer and in Great Britain in 1911 the Copyright Act was made. This guaranteed the composer's ownership, extending it to fifty years after the composer's death, during which time the composer's heirs became the copyright holders.

When a composer makes an agreement with a publisher, they share the ownership of the copyright. The publisher becomes the composer's agent whose duties may include printing the work, publicising it, distributing the orchestral and vocal parts to the performers, and generally looking after all the administrative work associated with the sale and performance of music. If the work is printed, the composer usually receives a payment or royalty on each copy sold.

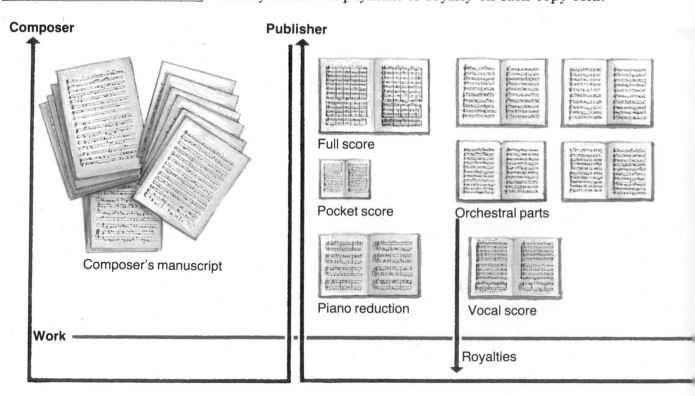

Composer

Publisher

Composer's manuscript

Full score

Pocket score

Orchestral parts

Piano reduction

Vocal score

Work

Royalties

For the complicated task of distributing the Performing Right Society's fees to its members, computers are used.

Below: A diagram showing the stages a piece of music might go through, from when it is first written, through its publication, to its performance and recording. The way in which royalties are distributed is also shown.

Performing Right

Composer and publisher share in the fees collected by the Performing Right Society. This organisation – and similar societies throughout the world – grants licences to perform music in public places such as pubs, restaurants, shops and halls, and to organisations such as radio and television companies. Fees are paid for these licences which are then divided between the member composers and publishers, according to the amount of each member's music that has been performed. Statements have to be obtained from the licensees as to what music they have been performing so that the Performing Right Society can distribute its revenue fairly. Licence fees vary enormously, that paid by the BBC, for example, being much larger than that paid by a small concert hall in a remote part of the country. The Performing Right scheme operates throughout the world, so that a copyright owner may expect to be paid, sooner or later, for works performed in places he or she may never have heard of.

A similar legal control governs the fees received from the sale of gramophone records (Mechanical Rights), which currently stand at a royalty of 6¼% of the sale price. Royalties on works written for the theatre are usually agreed individually with the theatre concerned and are known as Grand Right Works.

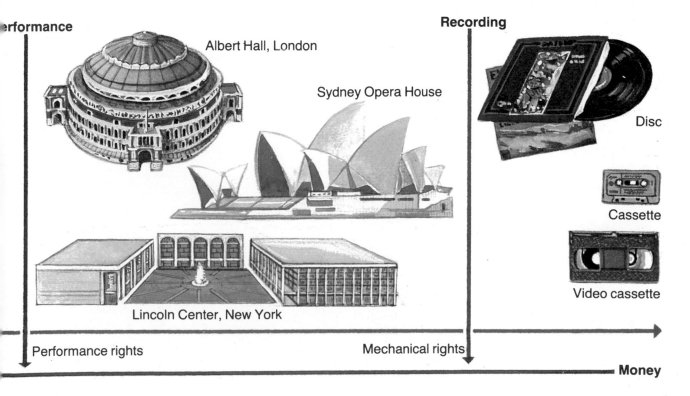

Performance

Albert Hall, London

Sydney Opera House

Lincoln Center, New York

Performance rights

Recording

Disc

Cassette

Video cassette

Mechanical rights

Money

Recording music

Record producer Christopher Bishop was recording the choir in King's College chapel, Cambridge, when 'Some birds settled on the west window and started twittering away, making a terrific din. It was audible on the record and we couldn't get rid of them. We tried firing guns at them and clapping but they wouldn't go. So we put a note on the record saying that anybody with very good ears and good equipment might be able to hear the sound of birds, and everybody immediately found they could hear it and thought that they must have wonderful ears and equipment.'

Music on record and tape has revolutionized people's attitudes and listening habits. Today it is possible not only to have music playing continuously but to hear a far greater variety of music than, say, a hundred years ago. Music from all periods of history and from all over the world can be heard.

As the recording industry has grown, techniques for obtaining the most accurate reproduction have become more and more complex. However, the methods of recording a piece of music, and the people involved, have remained more or less the same for the last few decades.

Responsibility for the final recording is shared equally between the producer and the conductor (if it is an orchestral piece) or individual players (if it is a solo or chamber work). The conductor is in charge of the performance from a musical point of view, and the producer is responsible for organizing and carrying through the recording, and making sure that it is of a high enough quality.

Recordings can take place in a studio, but often they are made in a room or hall not specially built for recording. This is because the room in which instruments are played has a great effect on their sound quality. It can make them sound very resonant, or very dry and dull. It is important, therefore, to choose a recording location with an acoustic to suit the music being recorded. A lot of church music, for example, is recorded actually in a church, because it makes it sound more resonant and closer to how it was originally heard.

Above: The conductor and record producer following scores of the music as they listen to the performance they have just recorded being played back. They are in a mobile studio because the recording session (right) is being held in a church.

When a piece of music is being recorded, it is normal for a long section, usually a movement, to be played through first without stopping. The conductor, record producer and balance engineer will then listen through and decide which passages need to be rerecorded, because of imperfections in playing or recording. The balance engineer may also make adjustments to the microphones. When there is a good enough recording of all the music, the tape editor takes over. Under direction from the producer, the editor cuts the tape and fits together the versions of the music considered to be the best. This is an extremely skilled job, as the joins in the tape must on no account be detectable by the listener.

Often recordings are made on a series of tracks, each with its own microphone covering a different instrument or instrumental group. The tracks are then mixed together and it is possible to readjust the balance of the recorded sounds during this process. Although this is done in making pop records, classical music is only rarely recorded in this way.

When operas are recorded, singers are moved around the studio floor so that the sound of their voices mainly comes out on one or other stereo channel. This makes recording more complicated as it is essential to note down where each singer is standing, so that if a passage has to be rerecorded he or she can be placed in the same position. Singers can also be moved artificially by recording them on separate tracks and adjusting their 'position' in the mixing process.

Once the master-tape has been made, the recorded sound can be turned into records or cassettes. Constant research is being carried out to improve the quality of reproduction, and recent developments have resulted in the compact disc and digital recording.

The conductor Giulini (seated in the centre of the picture), discussing a recording with the record producer and sound engineer

Above: A sound engineer seated at a mixing desk, controlling the levels at which the music is recorded. These are shown on the meters on the top of the desk.

Right: Seiji Ozawa indicating how he will conduct a particular moment in a piece by Andrzej Panufnik, seated on his right

The jazz composer

Scott Joplin, the 'father' of ragtime

Louis Armstrong's Hot 5. From left to right: Louis, Johnny St Cyr, Johnny Dodds, Edward 'Kid' Ory and Lil Hardin

Below: Ragtime composer J Russell Robinson is the pianist in this 1919 picture of the Original Dixieland Jazz Band, who had made the first jazz records two years before.

The early days

From the earliest days of jazz, the performer has been a composer, improvising the notes as they are played. But most jazz players improvise around tunes or chord sequences which have been written by a songwriter or composer. Gradually jazz composers started to write tunes especially for jazz players to improvise on. Improvisation involves making up tunes on the spur of the moment, and at first this was done as a group. The trumpeter played a lead, whilst clarinet and trombone made up supporting parts, and piano, bass and drums played an accompaniment.

In the days of ragtime, from the 1890s to the early 1920s, composers wrote both for ragtime piano players, and for small 'orchestras'. As well as the famous Scott Joplin, other composers such as J Russell Robinson and Artie Matthews wrote tunes which were used as the basis for improvisation, especially Matthews's famous *Weary Blues*.

By the time of the first gramophone records, jazz composers were arranging tunes to fit into the three-and-half-minute playing time of a 78 rpm record. Lil Hardin, the pianist, and her husband Louis Armstrong, arranged very simple backings for the long, exciting improvised solos of Armstrong's trumpet and Johnny Dodds's clarinet. These can be heard in the recordings of the Hot Five and Hot Seven from 1927, and marked the point when the improviser started to play alone, without other 'melody' instruments.

Also in 1927, the pianist Jelly Roll Morton, from New Orleans, was recording in Chicago with his Red Hot Peppers. Morton used simple orchestrations, unusual combinations of instruments, and varying rhythms to make each recorded side into a miniature composition, where the jazz soloist appeared in a carefully arranged instrumental framework. Tunes like *The Pearls* and *Sidewalk Blues* demonstrate this.

Jazz composer Jelly Roll Morton seen towards the end of his life while recording songs and piano solos for the US Library of Congress

Modern jazz composer, Tadd Dameron, who composed many of the tunes which made jazzmen Charlie Parker and Dizzy Gillespie famous

Right: Duke Ellington and Billy Strayhorn

Duke Ellington

The most influential jazz composer was Duke Ellington. He started composing for his big band at the Cotton Club in Harlem, New York, during the late 1920s, and like Morton recorded his work. But soon his compositions were spreading on to the larger twelve-inch discs, and often over more than one disc. From the start, his pieces were based on the particular soloists in his band. Later, he also used a wide and unusual range of instrumental combinations to extend his ideas, as well as composing for combinations of his sixteen-piece big band with symphony orchestras or choirs.

Duke was such a prolific composer he employed his own copyist to write out the parts for his musicians, and for much of his life he worked with the pianist and composer Billy Strayhorn, who travelled with the band. Between them, they wrote hundreds of pieces, and recorded many of them.

The start of modern jazz

In the 1940s a type of jazz called bebop developed which was more complicated and difficult to play than much that had gone before. Composers had to write new tunes for this new type of jazz, and many famous composers emerged, including Charles Mingus, Thelonious Monk, Gil Evans, Quincy Jones and Neal Hefti.

The arranger

Billy Strayhorn at work on a score after rehearsal. He started his career with Ellington at 23 as arranger and joint composer.

'An arranger is faced with arranging, and he's supposed to arrange *anything* according to what his style or talent is. If I'm working on a tune I don't want to *think* it's bad. It's just a tune, and I have to work with it.' Billy Strayhorn

Although Jelly Roll Morton and Duke Ellington arranged many of the tunes that they wrote, in order that they could be played by their own orchestras, other orchestras found that they needed arrangers to write versions of well-known tunes or compositions which would suit a particular combination of instruments. In order to make a setting for a jazz soloist to improvise in, the other players needed to play specially-written parts.

This is a skill which exists in classical music. Ravel's famous orchestration of Mussorgsky's piano piece *Pictures at an Exhibition* shows how adding instrumental tones and colouring to a work can alter and enrich it. In the eighteenth century, composers like Telemann and J S Bach rearranged works written for one instrument for another, or organ pieces for the orchestra.

Particular types of arrangements are needed for specialized music like film and television scores, and there is often the need to work at great speed in writing this kind of incidental music.

Right: Dizzy Gillespie, the jazz trumpeter, working on instrumental arrangements for his band during a recording session

Film and television composing

'The most difficult type of commission is films and television. You see the film through and you have to go home and start working immediately. You have to think of the right idea for the music straight off. You have no time for second thoughts.' John McCabe (above), who has written music for the film *Fear in the Night* and for several television programmes

Right: Studio musicians recording the music soundtrack by Sir William Walton for the famous Laurence Olivier film of *Hamlet*. The film was projected over the musicians' heads so that the conductor could time the musical sequences exactly. These days a television screen is almost always used.

Writing music for plays and films is a specialized job, because the music must be exactly the right length. The film or programme is usually made first, and watched by the composer, who notes down the action and mood in those sections for which music is required.

Many effects in films work because of the background music, which suggests mood, place, tension and so on. The instrumentation used can help tremendously, and sometimes unusual instruments are used together, producing a special atmosphere. Often there is a cost limitation, and composers have to write for a particular number of musicians.

Once the music has been written and arranged, it has to be recorded on to the soundtrack of the film or programme. Often this music is conducted by the composer or arranger so that last minute adjustments to the timing can be made during the recording, should the composer have written a few seconds too much or too little.

Composers such as Prokofiev and Copland have written film music, but many composers specialise in films, such as Bernard Hermann, John Williams and Erich Korngold.

The audience

All music has an audience, from folksongs to orchestral music, from opera to rock, and from films to records or tapes. Once the composer, arranger, publisher, performers, producer, engineers, printers and managers have done their jobs, then it is time for the audience to take over.

Audiences can be very important in determining the success of a piece of music, an orchestra, a conductor or a soloist. Without audiences the music business could not continue. But their judgement is not always reliable, and sometimes musicians and composers have defied public opinion and performed their work in the face of great opposition. In Paris in 1913 Stravinsky's *The Rite of Spring* caused an outraged audience to riot, but seventy years later it holds a central place in the orchestral repertoire. Equally, some composers popular in the last century are rarely heard these days.

London's Last Night of the Proms, in which the audience is encouraged to take part

Above: At a rock festival, the audience sits on the ground, or stands. They talk and move around freely.

Right: In the opera house, the audience is seated in rows on different levels, almost to the ceiling.